GREED
is not enough

GREED
is not enough

Reaganomics

ROBERT
LEKACHMAN

PANTHEON BOOKS NEW YORK

Library of Congress Cataloging in Publication Data

Lekachman, Robert.
Greed is not enough.

Includes index.
1. United States—Economic—1971–
2. Supply-side economics—United States.
I. Title.
HC106.7.L44   338.973   81–48228
ISBN 0–394–51023–2   AACR2

Manufactured in the United States of America

First Edition

For
E. W. L.

contents

ACKNOWLEDGMENTS

I salute first my publisher André Schiffrin, whose devotion to serious discussion of public issues reflects itself in each year's Pantheon list of new books. I owe a debt of gratitude to my admirable editor Phil Pochoda, whose candor and judgment I have come to admire even when critically exercised upon some of my most cherished words. Fairness compels me to add that without the inspiration of Ronald Reagan, I could never have completed this book.

GREED
is not enough

introduction

Enrichessez-vous.

ADVICE TO THE FRENCH FROM
FRANÇOIS PIERRE GUILLAUME GUIZOT,
CIRCA 1830

Ronald Reagan must be the nicest president who ever destroyed a union, tried to cut school lunch milk rations from six to four ounces, and compelled families in need of public help to first dispose of household goods in excess of $1,000.

This amiable gentleman's administration has been engaged in a massive redistribution of wealth and power for which the closest precedent is Franklin Roosevelt's New Deal, with the trifling difference that FDR sought to alleviate poverty and Ronald Reagan enthusiastically enriches further the already obscenely rich. Most of the benefits of 1981's tax legislation will flow to large corporations and their affluent stockholders, other prosperous individuals, commodity traders, military contractors, and truly greedy dabblers in oil, gas, and coal properties. Taxes on capital gains are sharply reduced. To all intents and purposes, levies on corporate profits are phasing themselves out. In future, estates passing to surviving spouses will be exempt from inheritance tax.

By more enlightened Western European and Scandinavian

criteria, the American welfare state is a ramshackle affair. Unemployment benefits are limited in duration and meager in amount. Comprehensive health care persists as a distant dream. Aid to families with dependent children (welfare) continues to be a patchwork of widely differing local benefit levels and eligibility definitions. In most jurisdictions, already inadequate benefits have lagged far behind inflation. Nevertheless, the administration's budget warriors concentrated most of their expenditure retrenchment upon Great Society programs designed to mitigate the misfortunes of the working poor, minorities, and welfare families.

In numerous ways, David Stockman and his helpers have also victimized the president's new blue-collar constituency, the 40 to 45 percent of factory workers who deserted Jimmy Carter and voted, usually for the first time in their adult lives, for a Republican presidential candidate. Massive White House retaliation against hapless air controllers[1] signaled a tough antiunion posture amply expressed in other ways. New members of the National Labor Relations Board come from the corporate community, not from congressional staffs, universities, or union associations. In private life a New Jersey building contractor, Secretary of Labor Raymond Donovan has been trying to erode the protection of union wage standards furnished by legislation originating in the 1930s.[2] His attempt, fortunately thwarted, to ease restrictions on industrial work performed at home, directly threatened the hard-won gains of unions in the garment trades.

Once upon a time Ronald Reagan headed the Screen Actors Guild. He retains his union card, admires Solidarity at a safe distance in Poland, and fervently endorses appropriately conducted collective bargaining. He broke the controllers' strike, decertified PATCO, and barred the strikers forevermore from

---

[1] The Professional Air Traffic Controllers Organization (PATCO) was one of a handful of unions which endorsed Reagan in 1980. The ingratitude of princes is notorious.
[2] The Davis-Bacon Act, a product of the *Hoover* Administration, requires that successful bidders for federal contracts pay prevailing wages to building craftsmen. "Prevailing" translates to union rates.

federal employment because they deserted their control towers illegally and violated their no-strike oath. What can a president do but enforce the law? Under equally plausible cover, Reagan's deregulators busily dismantle Occupational Safety and Health Administration efforts to protect factory employees against noxious chemicals, dangerous equipment, and noise levels destructive of hearing. What red-blooded American patiently tolerates red tape and bureaucratic interference, especially when corporate employers threaten to shut down rather than incur the costs imposed by OSHA, the Environmental Protection Administration, and other meddlers?

Even in prior Republican regimes, secretaries of the interior have habitually shielded national parks and other public lands from the more outrageous designs of developers, oil and gas explorers, lumbermen, and strip miners. By unrefreshing contrast, James Watt, fresh from his role as head of a public interest law firm representing precisely these interests, has openly enunciated plans to open as much of the public domain as he can possibly arrange to private exploitation. The Department of the Interior projects large transfers of public property to energy conglomerates and other corporate predators.

Much as 1981's tax and budget cuts hurt vulnerable individuals, Washington's defense plans and energy policies add to the problems of the troubled Northeast and industrial Midwest, and impart unneeded stimulus to the booming Southwest and Rocky Mountain states. The budget cuts afflict the older regions where large numbers of low-income families are concentrated and benefit standards are comparatively civilized. The economic benefits of new Pentagon contracts and deregulation of domestic oil prices are targeted to the lucky residents of the Sun Belt and the Rocky Mountain states. As ever, capital will flow out of stagnant regions and industries into places and activities that credibly promise higher returns on investment.

In a large and complicated polity like the United States, redistribution is never a simple matter of taking from those at the bottom of the income pyramid and giving to their financial betters. Some rich people stand to gain a great deal more than their social peers. Among them are the new energy multi- and centi-millionaires[3] of such states as Texas and Colorado and thriving entrepreneurs in the high technology of semiconductors, gene splicing, and robotics.

Prospects are distinctly less glowing for the owners of older money locked into troubled northern industries like rubber, glass, steel, and autos. Multinational corporations like General Motors and Ford, whose domestic operations, though decreasingly, have been historically concentrated in Michigan, Ohio, Illinois, and Indiana, have been afflicted by the crumbling structure of public services in Detroit, Cleveland, and other depressed midwestern centers. Sky-high interest rates on installment car purchases have plunged the industry into deep depression. Although the Reagan Administration negotiated "voluntary" restraints on Japanese exports, these did little good. The public could afford Toyotas and Hondas no more than it could Fords and Chevrolets.

The Reagan Administration usually means to help the business community, but its policies on occasion actually damage the interests of intended beneficiaries. While inflation has swelled the profits of sellers in expanding markets, it has acutely afflicted savings banks, savings and loan associations, life insurance companies, and bondholders and bond issuers. Thrift institutions that pay 5 1/2 percent interest lose vast sums to money market funds, Treasury bills, and other short-term federal securities.[4] Life insurers endure erosion in the market value of their bonds and debentures, for no sane individual would hold a twenty-year bond to maturity when the value of the dollars

---

[3]It is said that among the really rich, those who can claim assets of merely $5 or $10 million are scorned as five-and-dime types. During World War II, one London club for American officers excluded buck generals, owners of but a single star.

[4]The "All Savers" certificate, which allows banks to offer tax-free interest pegged at 70 percent of current Treasury bill rates, represented a congressional, not a White House, response to the threatened insolvency of numerous thrift institutions. It is a federal subsidy to the owners of bank stock.

in which it can be redeemed declines each year.

Savings bankers and life insurers tend to be sympathetic to Milton Friedman's monetarism because it offers hope of diminished inflation and ultimate return to price stability. When inflation runs in double digits, monetarists direct the Federal Reserve to slow the growth of money and credit and predict that interest rates will obediently decline as inflation expectations drain out of the economy.[5] In 1981, monetarist policy did little to diminish actual inflation and less to reduce anticipation of inflation in the future. Consequently, interest rates soared above 20 percent and conventional home mortgages, if available at all, averaged 17 percent by summer's end. As for the bond market, by the start of September 1981, a typical 25-year corporate bond, which traded at $1,063 on January 1, 1977, fetched a meager $457.36. In the same period, an 8 1/4 percent Treasury bond maturing in the year 2005 declined from $1,096 to $593. Felix Rohatyn of Lazard Frères, the investment bankers, and chairman of New York City's Municipal Assistance Corporation, who will reappear toward the end of this chronicle, divided the bond market into a "general disaster" sector of taxable corporate issues and the "total shambles" of municipal finance.[6]

This "total shambles" damages the financial health and stability of all the cities and states that are compelled to go to the bond markets for funds to finance capital projects, but as always the pain is unequally distributed. Houston needs money less and enjoys a better credit rating than New York. When it borrows, it is at rates lower than those that confront the Municipal Assistance Corporation as the metropolis's agent. In 1981, the New York State legislature belatedly authorized a large bond issue to rehabilitate the Big Apple's collapsing subways

---

[5] As the monetarist argument runs, high interest rates incorporate a premium against continued inflation demanded by lenders. When Citibank lends at 20 percent and anticipates 15 percent inflation, the inflation premium is three quarters of the rate charged and the true return to the lender a modest 5 percent.

[6] See *The New York Times,* September 11, 1981, pp. D 1, 7.

and buses. Because of punitive interest costs, the city has been compelled to stretch out its financing even though hopes of municipal revival require swift improvements in public transportation and other basic services.

As spender, regulator, contract dispenser, and taxer, the federal government dispenses benefits and inflicts losses that are anything but randomly allocated by geography, age, sex, income, or occupation. New York, Boston, Chicago, Philadelphia, and Cleveland lose larger sums per capita when Washington cuts back on rent subsidies, mass transit grants, assistance to schools in low-income districts, welfare allotments, school lunches, and food stamps than booming communities like Phoenix, Denver, Dallas, and Houston.

In the beleaguered Snow Belt, neither state nor local authorities dare raise taxes to replace federal subventions lest affluent individuals and major corporate employers take flight. At the same time, crumbling bridges and highways, bursting water mains, unreliable local electric utilities,[7] and inadequate levels of police, fire, and sanitation service encourage the mobile to move just as effectively as would higher taxes.

Other losers in the Reagan dispensation? Racism should be evaluated less by motive than by consequence. By this test, the Reagan Administration is the most racist in recent history. The limited gains registered by blacks and Hispanics in the last two decades are threatened, to begin with, by the administration's discrimination in favor of the Sun Belt. The large cities of the North are increasingly black and Hispanic. Accordingly, their misfortunes are those in particular of minorities. Rapid retreat from enforcement of affirmative action further dims the employment and promotion possibilities available to these groups.

Women also rank high among administration targets. Like blacks and Hispanics, they will suffer from the sabotage of

---

[7]For the third time since 1965, a Consolidated Edison power failure in September 1981 blacked out for several hours an area south of Times Square which included the computers of the financial community.

affirmative action. Low-income women will lose many benefits, among them the special nutritional allowances targeted at them and their young children. As far as educated female professionals are concerned, the nomination of Sandra O'Connor as the first female member of the Supreme Court symbolizes far more than a welcome breach in the male clubbiness of our highest court. Ms. O'Connor has had six years of judicial experience, all of them in the Arizona state courts. Several other women sit with distinction on federal benches, two or three of them at the circuit court level. There is reason to doubt that the president would have nominated a man with credentials as sketchy and it is still more doubtful that the Senate would have endorsed such a candidate if proposed. Ms. O'Connor is a token, an example less of sexism honorably resisted than of sexism adroitly indulged.

The president and his co-conspirators have been conducting undeclared war against blacks and Hispanics, welfare clients, women, children, and blue-collar workers. Under way is still another episode of class conflict between rich and poor. Americans are uncomfortable with the idea of social and economic class. No major politician, least of all virtuosos of sweet talk like the Republican leaders in Congress and the head man himself, entertains the notion of politics as class conflict. When the class served is the small but potent company of the rich and powerful, discretion is particularly advisable for its political allies.

HOW IT HAPPENED

How did a nice country like the United States collapse into the clutches of the reactionary political Right? Part of any answer concerns electoral arithmetic. Our voting participation rates amount to a durable scandal. In 1980, barely more than half the eligible electorate took the trouble to pull a lever for either loser or winner. The latter's "mandate" was conferred by a mere 28 percent of the electorate. As Walter Dean Burnham at the Massachusetts Institute of Technology has documented, the nonvoting half of the public belongs overwhelmingly—according to income, education, and occupational status—to groups that in Western European democracies vote on the left, for socialists and Communists in France and Italy, Labor candidates in England, and social democrats in Germany and Sweden.

Men and women who do not vote proclaim their indifference to or alienation from the electoral process. But because the natural partisans of social change opt out, progressive pressure upon the Democrats is exceedingly weak and both parties increasingly rely upon the corporate community for campaign funds and electoral support. If, for a time, Jimmy Carter was the favored instrument of the Trilateral Commission alliance of international bankers, industrial and service multinationals, Wall Street investment bankers, and out-of-season diplomats, it was because the Carter mixture of free trade, Keynesian economic stimulus, and mild welfarism appeared to guarantee expanding markets and rising profits, a return to the stable economic environment of the 1950s and the first half of the decade that followed. The second oil price shock in 1979 and the hostage crisis disordered international markets. Partly to meet their larger oil bills, the Japanese escalated their invasion of American consumer markets. As president, Jimmy Carter pursued wavering and inconsistent policies in both domestic and foreign affairs.

For liberal Democrats, the Carter Administration was an even graver disappointment. As a centrist in his party, Carter necessarily endorsed the Great Society agenda of sustained progress toward racial and sexual equality, federalization of welfare, comprehensive health care, and, most important of all, full employment. The last objective was entombed in the 1978 Humphrey-Hawkins Balanced Growth and Full Employment Act, a dead letter at the very moment Mr. Carter affixed to it his unenthusiastic signature.

Welfare reform and universal health coverage expired in Congress. Instead of full employment and rising living standards, blue-collar workers experienced layoffs and shrinkage of take-home pay. Their disappointment and frustration were exacerbated by the greatly exaggerated perception that taxes deducted from their hard-earned paychecks were mostly transferred to lazy and profligate welfare families and the bureaucrats who indulged them. When times are bad, the wellsprings of compassion quickly dry up. Within the social welfare fraternity, it is axiomatic that programs for poor people tend to be poor programs—inadequately funded, intrusively administered, and widely resented by the majority of the population who are ineligible for their benefits. From the bleak perspective of families not much better off than the beneficiaries of food stamps, Medicaid, and other programs, the logical alternative reforms were either extension of such income supplements to the employed working class or the population at large, or curtailment of subsidies to current recipients.

The alternatives existed more in hypotheses than in practical politics. The only major political figure who strongly favored widening of housing and welfare programs and universalization of health protection was Teddy Kennedy, who lost his primary bid against a sitting president who used the hostage crisis to his own competitive advantage. In November 1980, the actual choice presented to wage earners was between retention of a president and an administration that had cost them income and job opportunities, and a candidate whose appeal was couched in inspiringly affirmative language. Ronald Reagan promised more jobs, rising take-home pay, lower taxes, and less inflation.

Some students of public opinion believe that Reagan turned probable victory into landslide at the moment he peered candidly at the cameras in his debate with Carter and uttered a devastating challenge: "Ask yourself if you are better off than you were four years ago." No threat of class war, no intimation of anti-union sentiment, no suggestion of assault upon Social Security or unemployment compensation, even subliminally tinged the candidate's accents. As the least ideological of unions in the industrialized portion of the world, the AFL-CIO heard in Reagan's appeal echoes of its own song. Like union leaders, the man simply sought more money, better benefits, and increased job opportunities.

The history of American industrial relations is dotted with episodes of violent employer resistance to the organizational efforts of unions. But in the quarter century of steady economic growth after World War II, détente between major unions and leading corporate employers characterized contract negotiations and day-to-day factory relations between supervisors and union representatives. For, when growth is buoyant, issues of equity in the distribution of its proceeds recede into the background and agitate mere handfuls of disaffected intellectuals. Growth enlarges the number of winners. Expansion makes promotion more frequent, but even a man or woman stuck at a median income figure fares better each year as that median rises.

The astute 1980 Republican campaign and the party's carefully programmed national candidates deployed the lure of renewed growth as an effective cloak for policies certain to aggravate existing inequities in the distribution of income and wealth between whites and minorities and men and women. For successful candidates, growth is a unifying theme. In 1968, even Richard Nixon, that most divisive of presidents, presented himself as a peacemaker destined to bring Americans together again. Like Lyndon Johnson, chief executives tend to bill themselves as presidents of all the people.

Supply-Side Magic

For the cynical public, a candidate needs to make his promises credible. The Republicans presented supply-side economics as a wide-spectrum antibiotic, absolutely certain to cure the economy of its infectious fevers and stimulate the patient to prodigies of effort. Supply-side arguments will merit frequent attention in the pages that follow, but a few words of preliminary exegesis seem appropriate. In pure form, supply-side economics is an assertedly powerful relationship between tax rates and incentives to work, save, and invest, in free market economies where, for the most part, factories, retail establishments, and banks are privately owned.

In such communities, entrepreneurs can legally start new enterprises, enlarge existing units, or shut down and retire to Florida. Wage earners divide their paychecks between spending and saving as they list. Similarly, they can choose between added income and leisure, between overtime pay and a day on the beach. On the Wednesday afternoons habitually dedicated to golf, doctors and dentists can instead treat more patients.

Economists believe in human rationality. We work harder for larger rewards. We incur the risks of investment when the potential return outweighs the danger of loss. We save our money only out of the calculation that the interest earned will exceed the inflation rate. When the rewards of overtime work are taxed more steeply, men and women prefer leisure to what is left as added income[8] after IRS does its thing. Why save if interest earned is heavily taxed? What's the point of gambling on a risky investment if the tax collectors reap a large share of eventual profit and refuse to share in losses?

The Laffer curve (of which more later), portrays the truism that a 100 percent tax on earnings will generate universal idleness and zero tax revenue. Since all taxes discourage the activities to which they apply, the challenge to enlightened public officials is to select the very lowest tax rates compatible with funding of essential government activities. The less progressive the taxes on personal incomes can be made, the smaller the penalty imposed upon talented and productive individuals who populate the upper reaches of the income distribution.

From here on, we require faith. Supply-siders *know* that

---

[8]A progressive tax, like that on personal income, imposes rising rates on additions to earnings. A prudent soul accordingly focuses his attention upon the rate which applies to any additional dollars he might acquire.

American taxes are too high, in particular those that apply to the incomes of the more successful. As a fruit of similar inspiration, they are certain that the original Kemp-Roth schedule of 10 percent cuts in personal income levies for three years is just the formula to inspire a surge of new investment, a revival of thrift, and a renewal of a Calvinist work ethic eroded but happily not destroyed by the misguided egalitarianism of the Democrats. In the most cheerful version of supply-side gospel, the booming Gross National Product will restore, and more than restore, government receipts temporarily lost because of tax reduction. Until the awesome mantle of administrative responsibility descended upon their shoulders, supply-siders worried very little about temporary deficits and were comparatively gentle in their prescriptions for surgery upon the social heritage of the New Deal and Great Society.

Such is the argument immortalized in supply-side scripture.[9] As ever, politics and economic events are far more complicated than the pieties of popular theology. Innocent like most politicians of economic expertise, Mr. Reagan as candidate and occasional tenant of the Oval Office has ecumenically welcomed aboard the ship of state two rival conservative coteries. There are, to start with, the monetarists, inspired by Milton Friedman and notably represented in Washington by Treasury Undersecretary Beryl Sprinkel and Federal Reserve Chairman Paul Volcker. Monetarists believe that money matters. Who of us does not? They go much further: they assert that money is the only economic variable that does matter. The key to price stability, steady growth at inspiring rates, rising standards of life, and extermination of the Mediterranean fruit fly, is obedience on the part of the money managers, our much maligned Federal Reserve, to a single rule. The Fed must take care to

---

[9]For those of religious inclination, the three holy books are Jude Wanniski's *The Way the World Works* (1978), Jack Kemp's *An American Renaissance* (1979), and George Gilder's *Wealth and Poverty* (1981), all three published by Basic Books, New York. Gilder's polemic placed high on the best-seller list for months.

enlarge the quantity of money and credit no faster than the growth of GNP, say 3 percent each year. Each time the Fed meddles with interest rates and tries to promote recovery from recession, it incurs the guilt of hubris by substituting its own judgment for that of the free market.

On the day that the Fed convinces consumers and investors that it has mastered the monetarist lesson, inflation expectations will drain out of the national psyche, and all of us, breathing a collective sigh of relief, will be able to concentrate upon the real stuff of material life—buying and selling, working and earning, saving and investing.

Like other performers in the tragicomedy of Reaganomics, monetarists will enter and exit frequently as the tale unfolds. Yet a third set of actors jostle supply-siders and monetarists for the president's brief span of attention. They are the old-fashioned balanced-budget conservatives, among them Herbert Stein and Alan Greenspan, successive chairmen of the Nixon-Ford Council of Economic Advisers, George Schultz, a Nixon treasury secretary, and that good, gray personage Arthur F. Burns, Eisenhower's head of the Council of Economic Advisers, Nixon's chairman of the Federal Reserve, and, now in his late seventies, Reagan's ambassador to Bonn. These men of large affairs view monetarists and supply-siders with a certain salutary skepticism. Although they share the preferences of both groups for smaller government and less regulation of private activity, they prefer to shrink government directly by reducing spending before cutting taxes. Good children eat their vegetables before lapping up their ice cream. As faithful Republican loyalists, the budget balancers have uttered their doubts *sotto voce* and, in public, affirmed their belief in the soundness of administration policies.

What are these policies? Not for the first time, a president, having been offered conflicting counsel by his supporters, has embraced all of their recommendations and blessed impartially the conflicting theories from which they sprang. Supply-siders got their heart's desire, an approximation of the Kemp-Roth tax cuts. Monetarists fared even better. The administration, with only occasional backsliding, encouraged the Fed to persevere in tight money policies—however these might affect builders, automobile dealers, and small businessmen crunched by destructive interest rates. The budget balancers were offered the sop of $36 billion of reductions in the 1982 budget and promises of larger cuts to come.

When, at the beginning of August 1981, Ronald Reagan left Washington for a month of horseback riding, woodchopping, and brush clearing on his California ranch, he seemed emperor of all he deigned to survey. Cowed by the crack of the White House whip, Congress obediently accepted the administration's tax scheme and sabotaged, according to orders, two generations of social legislation. A month later, when the president revisited the White House, the political weather had turned foul. A storm of complaint about high interest rates reverberated in the ears of senators and congresspersons who had spent their summer recess in communion with the folks back home. Constituent distress complemented disorder on Wall Street. For the moment, it was hard to find a broker who believed in supply-side economics.

For connoisseurs of political comedy, the screams from the Reagan camp were the best of fun and Senator Howard Baker the most admired of thespians. This even-tempered, impeccably conservative soul grumbled about misbehavior on Wall Street, shared dark suspicions of conspiracy,[10] and threatened dreadful reprisals if the brokers and traders didn't straighten up and act like true believers. What fun to hear a responsible Republican contemplate credit allocation, taxes on income from interest, and wage and price controls. The spectacle of the Republican Senate majority leader as a closet Galbraithian lightened the gloom of the political scene.

---

[10]One indignant panelist on public television's popular "Wall Street Week" wondered how anybody believed that securities traders were conspiring to lose money.

WHAT NEXT?

One must cry for the victims of brutal social policy, and resist infliction of further suffering upon vulnerable Americans, but mirth cannot be avoided at the adverse verdict of the corporate and financial community upon the conduct of the most pro-business chief executive since Calvin Coolidge.

The failure of Reagan economic policy was readily predictable. Supply-side policies clash directly with monetarism. The success of the former requires easy credit, low interest rates, and a resulting boom in investment. Monetarism can slaughter the inflation dragon only by starving the economy of funds for new machines and factories, and keeping interest rates high enough for long enough to shove the economy into a good, old-fashioned recession. Painful as the budget cuts were for low-income Americans, they were much smaller than the projected increases in Pentagon appropriations. Who could believe that the budget really would be balanced in 1984?

Even before Congress returned to work after Labor Day 1981, troubled supply-siders like Jude Wanniski and Arthur Laffer[11] were searching desperately for a *deus ex machina* to salvage the supply-side experiment. In urgent tones, they called for a return to the gold standard—the free exchange of paper money for gold. The gold standard, as the argument goes, is the best insurance against inflation because as soon as the Fed prints too much money, the public will turn it into gold. The gold drain will compel the Fed to restrict credit, and people with gold will sell it for dollars of increasing value.

Ever obliging, the president duly appointed a gold commission to evaluate the case for a return to the gold standard. Its members were more or less equally divided among gold standard enthusiasts like Lewis Lehrman, monetarists like Federal

---

[11]Although Laffer has inspired Wanniski, Kemp, and Gilder to expound supply-side theory at book length, he has, to his credit, written no book of his own. According to legend, he drew the first Laffer curve on a restaurant napkin.

Reserve Governor Henry Wallich, and neutrals like Treasury Secretary Donald T. Regan. As one business journal temperately editorialized, "There is no way that either the U. S. or the world can find its way back to the gold standard that existed before World War I. That system was partly a state of mind and partly a creation of the Bank of England which dominated international credit. Lost innocence cannot be restored. The discipline of the old gold standard cannot be re-established because central banks know that the world will not come to an end if they cannot redeem their currencies in gold."[12]

The gold standard broke down in the first place because the publics of Western democracies were no longer willing to tolerate the recessions and financial crises that adherence to the gold standard repeatedly entailed. Its disinterment signalizes the desperation within the Reagan camp.

The administration cannot escape painful identification of its priorities. If the Russians really are scrambling through the "window of vulnerability" that chiefs of staff and defense intellectuals fret over, then the United States must tool up the economy as for a protracted, armed conflict. Any version of a national security state requires controls over prices and incomes, rationing of vital raw materials, and confrontation with the Soviets and their surrogates in the Middle East, Africa, and Latin America. It need hardly be said that the national security state spells finis to supply-side management of the economy.

The best way to reduce federal spending and resulting deficits is to perform radical surgery on the Pentagon, not the cosmetic trims acceptable to Defense Secretary Casper Weinberger. To put the economy first and defense second or lower is politically expensive for this president. Such a policy shift necessitates abandonment of the administration's treasured bipolar vision of international politics as a Manichean conflict between the forces of light and the devil's army of the night. It implicitly accepts the world as the stage of tangled affections and rivalries.

---

[12]See *Business Week,* September 21, 1981, p. 144.

Pakistanis hate Indians more sincerely than Russians. The Saudis take the threat of Zionism more seriously than the menace of communism. Black Africa is obsessed by apartheid rather than great power rivalries.

Where else can the president's helpers locate the huge budget cuts apparently essential to the revival of Wall Street confidence? A little more money can be squeezed out of Medicaid, food stamps, federal assistance to schools in the urban slums, and similar ventures. However, the only source of large savings is Social Security. Ronald Reagan just might balance the 1984 budget and enlarge the Pentagon, if he breaks his promises to the pensioners.

In the remainder of this administration, the most fascinating politics will play themselves out within the business community. Important sectors of that community—major defense contractors and energy conglomerates—share hawkish perceptions of international affairs and definitions of defense necessities.

Theirs is not the only important current of business opinion. Quiet for the moment, but likely to become more vocal as the unsatisfactory performance of the economy continues, is the planning wing of the business community. In 1976, a number of important business leaders[13] joined intellectuals on the moderate left[14] to explore the topic of national economic planning. The fruits of their deliberations were a statute entitled the National Economic Planning Act of 1976, subsequently sponsored in the Senate, in somewhat altered form, by the late Hubert Humphrey and Jacob Javits. Planners in the corporate interest cherish lingering affections for détente as having been good for business. Their preference for orderly domestic policy

---

[13]Among them were W. Michael Blumenthal, at the time head of Bendix and later Carter's treasury secretary, J. Irwin Miller of Cummins Engine, and Robert Roosa, an investment banker who served President Kennedy as undersecretary of the treasury. Henry Ford II expressed sympathy for the enterprise.

[14]Nobel Laureate Wassily Leontieff, John Kenneth Galbraith, Robert Heilbroner, and I were among the members.

at home translates into substantial federal direction of the economy.

In a fluid political and economic situation, no one can sensibly forecast this uniquely reactionary administration's next phase of policy. One prediction is safe: What the Reagan regime attempts in 1983 and 1984 will resemble its 1981 actions as distantly as Carter's promises matched his achievements.

Already Democrats have the chance to apply Ronald Reagan's challenge to its author: Are you better off now than in January 1977? If the president were unwise enough to borrow New York Mayor Edward Koch's incessant query, "How'm I doing?", the candid retorts might well offend the Moral Majority and defy publication in the *New York Times.*

new men,
new directions

As distinguished from the inspirational rhetoric out of Reagan's Washington about safety nets, the truly needy, and the asserted habit of rising tides lifting all boats, real politics, as ever, is about money. Annual budget traumas at all levels of government register the agonizing process of distributing among many claimants the community's output of necessary and desirable goods and services—food and shelter, underwear and fuel, automobiles and appliances, blue jeans and stereos, drugs and booze, an endless roster of temptations dangled by merchandisers before mass clienteles.

In one manner or another, cities, counties, states, and the federal establishment spend roughly a third of the American Gross National Product, or in round numbers a cool trillion dollars. How the politicians allocate such an incomprehensible sum powerfully shapes the relative fortunes of young workers and pensioners; the poor, the middle class, and the genuinely affluent; men and women; booming Sun Belt and sagging Frost

Belt; whites, blacks, and Hispanics; cities and suburbs; farmers and consumers; giant corporations and small businesses; and Americans and foreigners.

When economic growth is slow or negligible (the recent American condition), politicians cannot indulge themselves by dividing up among practically all clamoring groups swelling revenue from rapidly rising annual output and income. Since the end of the 1960s, output has risen only slowly and revenue accordingly has refused to swell. In choosing to spend money on some people, some places, and some programs, Congress must painfully refrain from directing elsewhere the benign stream of public expenditure. More for cities, poor people, minorities, and senior citizens inevitably diminishes benefits targeted to suburbs, prosperous families, the white majority, and the young. Politicians remain in office by avoiding choice. Successful practitioners of the art of governance in democracies much prefer as a grammatical locution "both . . . and" to "either . . . or." Circumstances not of their own devising have compelled them to choose.

Like public spending, the taxes collected to pay for it influence the distribution of income and wealth. The kind of taxes imposed, the rates at which they are collected, and the nature of the exemptions and deductions permitted, enrich some, add to the burdens of others, and almost invariably inflict heavier burdens upon some taxpayers than others even when their incomes are similar. Large families fare better than small ones. Home owners come out ahead of renters. Recipients of capital gains pay lower taxes than those who receive the same sums as wages or salaries.

The United States is a conservative country. Democrats and Republicans are invariably considerate of affluent individuals and the business community, the major sources of campaign funding. Candidates like George McGovern and Fred Harris, who favor mild redistribution of income and wealth, risk premature retirement by the voters. After the 1976 race, Fred Harris became a professor of government at the University of

New Mexico in accordance with the strange academic opinion that defeated politicians are the best guides for young men and women who aspire to understand the government of their country. For his part, George McGovern, in the wake of his 1980 defeat, joined the ranks of lobbyists for good causes in Washington.

Nevertheless, ever since the New Deal, Democrats have also been attentive to the needs of other constituencies, among them the poor, the elderly, the black, and the urban who have repaid such concern in the coin of votes. Republicans in their spells of national office have almost invariably been compelled to accept what the Democrats have wrought by the fact of Congresses controlled by their opponents.

The Congress elected in 1980, for the first time since 1946 is solidly conservative, formally in the Senate where Republicans are a majority, and factually in the House now dominated by a coalition of Republicans and "boll weevils," as conservative southern Democrats proudly nickname themselves. The second important difference between the Reagan and the Nixon-Ford regime is a matter of personality. Even when Nixon set out to do a good deed, as in the instance of his welfare reform proposal, he clothed his intentions in harsh, punitive rhetoric, and denials of altruistic aspirations. How different is Ronald Reagan, that exceptionally appealing human being, amiable to all, malicious to none, genuinely courageous in the presence of personal danger, and endowed with a repertory of one-liners that masquerades successfully as humor. Few doubt the sincerity of this fine man's belief that his program will restore roses to the cheeks of the American economy. In the vibrant future, minorities and the poor will improve their condition like luckier Americans. If the Great Society has created a class of welfare junkies, if government regulation of air quality, product quality, drug reliability, equal opportunity hiring, and workplace safety, among other good causes, has discouraged investment and dampened entrepreneurial spirits, then the right way, the only effective way genuinely to aid welfare clients and factory workers, is to reduce benefits for the former and federal interference with the employers of the latter. Ours is a time when, in order ultimately to be kind, it is necessary temporarily to be cruel. Such is the message enunciated in sweet, smiling tones by the president of the United States.

The Reagan manner clothes a political initiative unique in our national history: a quite deliberate redirection of income and wealth from the poor to the rich; blacks and Hispanics to whites; women to men; the elderly to the young; old, declining regions to booming Sun Belt cities; and social services to the Pentagon. Within the business community, Reagan's candidacy drew its strongest supporters from hawkish members of the defense contracting and energy community. Although the business community in general has retreated from its earlier enthusiasm for trade with the Russians in the first days of détente, differences persist over the desirable temperature of a new cold war and the consequent scale of Pentagon expansion. The differences are epitomized in Carter's projected 5 percent build-up and Reagan's promise of 7 percent. During the period between his retirement from politics and his emergence as a major California politician, Ronald Reagan toured the lecture circuit on behalf of General Electric, preaching the hard line anti-Communism which is at the core of his convictions. It seems likely that supply-side economics serves the traditional function of ideology in providing suitable cover for the pursuit of specific financial and commercial interests. In Reagan's coalition these are geographically concentrated in the Southwest, Far West, and Mountain states. Among businessmen his favorites are self-made entrepreneurs who comprise his kitchen cabinet. More specifically, supply-side economics during the presidential campaign reconciled in appearance simultaneous Pentagon build-up, major tax reduction, and rapid deregulation, and discreetly concealed the tremendous shifts of income and wealth from older to newer enterprises, from producers for the civilian market to the defense sector, and from the North to the South.

There have been other periods when this country devoted itself exclusively to the nurture of the affluent, most recently in the Coolidge era. In the 1920s, the federal government was a small presence, not the massive operator it became after several wars and two spells of social progress, the New Deal and the Great Society. With the worst will in the world, Republicans half a century ago could not curtail welfare, unemployment benefits, free medical care for the medically indigent, and Social Security. None of these modest protections yet ruffled the susceptibilities of industrialists and bankers.[1]

Since then, Americans have traveled in the direction taken by Western Europe and Scandinavia long before them. Like other inhabitants of moderately civilized communities, Americans expect shelter from the misfortunes of severe illness, disabling accident, unemployment, and indigent old age. Usually with little enthusiasm, conservatives take the permanence of these shelters for granted. The more intelligent of their number regard social expenditure as the price of social stability. Conservatives habitually emphasize frugal administration of existing programs and caution in the addition of new ones. Eisenhower, Nixon, and Ford, Reagan's three Republican predecessors, were conservatives firmly in this ideological mold.

Ronald Reagan is no conservative. He is, in the dictionary meaning of the word, a reactionary, intent upon a return to an earlier and more desirable set of relationships between citizens and their government. He is unique: the first reactionary American president.

This vision of historical retrogression is implicit in the details of *A Program for Economic Recovery,* David Stockman's "black book" of budget cuts issued less than a month after the new administration came into power. That program is as implausible in its economic assumptions as it is inequitable in its impact.

---

[1] See a useful essay by Thomas Ferguson and Joel Rogers, "The Reagan Victory: Corporate Coalitions in the 1980 Campaign" in *The Hidden Election*, edited by the two authors of this essay (Pantheon, 1981).

I postpone for a space the close inquiry it merits to say something about the intellectual origins of supply-side revelation.

II

In the beginning, that eighteenth-century dawn of Adam Smith and the school of classical economists who amplified his doctrines in the next century, all economists operated on the supply side. The economic problem was the alleviation of scarcity and improvement of the condition of the average Englishman. Only the truly wealthy, a tiny fraction of the public, enjoyed incomes substantial enough to subject their recipients to the agonies of choice in its spending. Most people staggered along from day to day on the edge of destitution, able to purchase no more than the bare necessities of survival. Eighteenth-century writers revealingly described farm and factory workers as "the poor."

Accordingly, it was the commonest of sense for friends of humanity to focus upon supply. The masses could lead better lives only as they became more efficient and produced continuously expanding amounts of product per person. *The Wealth of Nations* was a massive treatise about the sources of material wealth. A moral philosopher by trade, Adam Smith based his analysis upon two crucial propositions. The first was psychological. All human beings intelligently pursued their self-interest. Workers sought higher wages no less avidly than their employers pursued larger profits. The prospect of better pay lured alert men and women from less rewarding employment, just as the expectation of plumper profits attracted entrepreneurs into growing industries and accelerated their departure from those that were stagnating or shrinking.

Smith's equally central second proposition was technical, the close association between rising productivity and division of labor. The more finely industrial processes were divided and subdivided, the more substantial were the rewards in worker dexterity, the smaller the fraction of the working day wasted in sauntering from one task to another, and the more fertile the soil for the sprouting of labor-saving inventions. From this pair of generalizations, Smith drew momentous inferences. To begin with, when the restraints upon individual action were least, self-interest flourished most lushly. Smith sternly criticized the mercantilists of his own time for their misguided attempts to regulate wages, access to skilled trades, imports, domestic prices, and the internal migration of ambitious men and women.

Providentially, the self-interest of individuals coincides with the welfare of the public, as though an "invisible hand" were at work. Manufacturers and merchants selfishly crave as many customers as they can coax into disbursement. They would gladly sell adulterated merchandise at exorbitant prices, if only they could. Competition compels each seller to furnish decent quality at reasonable prices, for, just offstage, clamorous rivals wait in the wings for the chance to lure away dissatisfied customers.

For Smith, there was an additional point of great consequence. As measured by rising per capita output, efficiency and spreading division of labor could advance only as markets widened. Thinly populated communities cannot support specialists. In such places, farmers must shoe their own horses, fix their own roofs, sharpen their own implements, and medicate their families and domestic animals because no specialist could rationally expect to make a living there. Market size is a matter partly of population density and partly of the quality of transportation. Here government has a proper role. It should build roads and improve harbors because ease of travel for people and merchandise promotes specialization and ever more intricate divisions of labor.

Nevertheless, the general prescription was laissez faire, free trade among nations and within each of them. Governments were charged with the administration of justice and the defense of the realm. For the rest, the less they interfered in the affairs of their constituents the better for the political and economic health of society.

Until the 1870s, respectable economists in the English-speaking world concentrated on improvement of Smith's vision and modification of its technical expression. To the considerable extent that economists influenced English public policy, it was invariably in the direction of diminished public interference with private economic actions. The symbol of laissez faire's triumph was parliamentary repeal in 1846 of the Corn Laws which for centuries had shielded English farmers from the competition of foreign producers.

Laissez faire naturally extended to the workplace. Adult males,[2] by hypothesis the best judges of their own interests, could be depended upon to negotiate astutely wages and working conditions and, if displeased with what was offered, pull up stakes and move to more active labor markets.

In the factories of the Industrial Revolution, life was a grim affair. Protracted spells of unemployment during recurrent business-cycle depressions compelled workers and their families to throw themselves on the untender mercies of local welfare administrators. Nevertheless, living standards did rise during the nineteenth century. Human history never ought to be confused with the controlled experiments of laboratory science, but at least English adoption of laissez faire coincided with, if it did not cause, the spurt of investment, invention, foreign trade, and entrepreneurial vigor that turned Great Britain into the workshop of the world, as much the globe's dominant economy as, for a generation after World War II, the United States was in the twentieth century.

Diffusion of prosperity to an increasing middle class and even skilled factory workers modified the exclusive emphasis upon supply of English economics. Affluence connotes choice. Although, by the criteria of the 1980s, average families were worse

---

[2]True believers like John Stuart Mill reluctantly agreed that children and women were proper objects of concern for government. Because the former were too young to be rational and the latter were unjustly subordinated to men, neither group could deal as equals with potential employers. Hence, regulation of hours and working conditions was appropriate, but never for full-grown men.

off than contemporary welfare recipients, men and women contrasted thankfully their condition with that of their parents and
grandparents and found cause for celebration.
That celebration gave economists a new topic: the analysis of
demand. After they buy the necessities of daily life, how do
consumers choose to spend the rest of their earnings? To this
day, economists brood with loving subtlety over the intricacies
of consumer behavior. But the new emphasis, dignified by his-
torians of economic ideas as the "marginalist revolution,"[3]
complemented older doctrine, rather than supplanted it. Although, by the end of the nineteenth century, textbooks had
begun to parallel chapters on supply with usually shorter dis-
cussions on demand, the dominant view was that of Alfred
Marshall, the leading economist of the late nineteenth and early
twentieth century. He was certain that economic growth and
the hope of general affluence flowed not from the cravings of
consumers for higher living standards but from the restless
activities of entrepreneurs and the ambitions of their employees
for better wages. Activities, not wants, shape an economy and
determine its prospects.

Strong faith perennially resists distressing evidence of irrele-
vance or inadequacy. Thoroughly socialized economists never
doubted that laissez faire was the policy for all places and all
seasons. Nevertheless, England herself pursued free trade only
for the half century when the policy coincided with the interests
of employers eager to exploit new markets for their exports
while importing the cheapest available food, the better to keep
down both living costs and wages. The United States and Bis-
marck's Germany ignored conventional economic wisdom and
protected their infant industries from English extinction with
high tariffs.

Again in Germany, the theology of laissez faire gave ground

---

[3]Focusing on the spending habits of consumers, the marginalists of the final three
decades of the nineteenth century argued that rational men and women scrupulously
compared the extra or "marginal" pleasure to be expected from a purchase with the
extra or "marginal" dollars spent to acquire it.

to the realities of industrial society. How could an ordinary wage slave really protect himself from unemployment, indigence in old age, and catastrophic illness? Germany in the 1880s and England a decade later initiated the modern welfare state with modest pensions for the elderly and limited public subsidy of health care.

Other weeds grew in the economists' utopia. In market after market, large corporations, cartels, and monopolies weakened or destroyed the fierce competition among sellers which protected buyers from extortion and impelled entrepreneurs to improve quality and increase efficiency. Economists might dream about numerous small enterprises in constant rivalry. The truth was elsewhere. The economies of scale associated with mass production required massive investment and limited the number of producers who could operate profitably.

World War I completed the demolition of laissez faire. The Treaty of Versailles disrupted world trade and the delicate fabric of the international division of labor. Germany's new boundaries separated her from the coal and iron ore of Silesia and Alsace-Lorraine. Successor states to the Austro-Hungarian Empire—Hungary, Czechoslovakia, and Yugoslavia—pursued protectionist policies. Along the frontier of the new Soviet Union were free Poland, Finland, and the Baltic states of Lithuania, Latvia, and Estonia.

The United States and Western Europe enjoyed a false prosperity during the 1920s, on the flimsy foundation of a structure of international debt certain to collapse under its own weight. England and France could repay the huge sums they had borrowed from the United States to finance wartime purchases of food and munitions only by extracting similar amounts from the vanquished Germans. But the economically depleted Germans could hope to finance their reparations only from export earnings of unprecedented size. Confronted with their own difficulties of demobilization, no major importing country, least of all the United States, was willing to allow German merchandise unimpeded entry.

Evasion is the normal response as much to public as to personal difficulty. In the 1920s, evasion took the shape of American loans to Germany. The large sums made available to the Germans under the terms of the Dawes and Young agreements enabled the German government to pay the European winners on time. They in turn honorably remitted successive installments of interest and principal. The illusory process could continue only so long as all the parties to it ignored linkages among the financial flows, and American bankers in particular refused to note that the hundreds of millions of dollars traveling east to the Germans were the source of the hundreds of millions of dollars moving west to the Americans. The Germans could no more fulfill reparations obligations out of their own export earnings than in our own time the developing lands of the Third World can repay Citibank and Chase Manhattan.

Thus, even before the 1929 crash and the deep depression which ensued in the next decade, free trade had vanished. With the exception of the United States, all major industrial societies were enlarging the scope of the welfare state. Everywhere large economic units—giant corporations and large trade unions—were supplanting old-fashioned competitive markets.

Alert to these trends, prescient economists began to question the validity of received wisdom. In 1926, John Maynard Keynes, the boldest of these spirits, published *The End of Laissez-Faire,* a pamphlet that justified its ominous title by emphasis upon the emergent role of large corporations as entities intermediate between maximizing individuals and meddling public administrators. Anticipating the argument advanced a few years later by A. A. Berle and Gardner Means in the classic *The Modern Corporation and Private Property,*[4] Keynes identified increasing separation of ownership and management and speculated that "the general stability and reputation of the institution are more considered by the management

---

[4] New York: Macmillan Co., 1931.

than the maximum of profit for the shareholders." In Keynes's judgment, as competition declined, more and more of the English economy was becoming semisocialized.

Another decade elapsed before Keynes was prepared to offer the world an alternative theory, an explanation that really could replace supply with demand as the clue to comprehension of prosperity and depression. The cataclysm of massive, protracted, apparently interminable depression imparted urgency to Keynes's search for a satisfying analysis. Hordes of idle workers, scores of industrial ghost towns, thousands upon thousands of bankrupt merchants and expropriated family farmers gave the lie to assurances from the learned that the business cycle was a self-correcting phenomenon, and rendered as hollow as the bellies of ill-nourished Depression casualties the expert's counsel to avoid hasty government intervention and persevere in prudent budget-balancing tactics. Pragmatic politicians like Franklin Roosevelt, recipient of a gentleman's C— in economics at Harvard, hired unemployed men and women, put the young to work in Civilian Conservation Corps camps, subsidized farmers and home owners, and financed new roads and public buildings without much worry about consequent deficits in national budgets.

There comes a moment when even the most fervent of faiths surrenders to massive events. Even before Keynes in 1936 published *The General Theory of Employment, Interest and Money,* economists were losing their confidence in the principles upon which they had been raised. Yet, for lack of alternatives, they continued to teach and advocate doctrines and policies to which they were less and less devoted. They were followers awaiting a leader, true believers in search of fresh revelation.

Care must be taken in retelling briefly the familiar chronicle of Keynesian triumph. The man himself was no revolutionary. With a sniff of Bloomsbury disdain, he dismissed all versions of Marxism as intellectually contemptible. Although at times he sounded like a democratic socialist, his basic message was one of guidance to bewildered politicians in their attempts to prop up and resuscitate the capitalist invalid.

Any genuinely important theory must sustain the test of brief, even platitudinous summary. Much as the theory of evolution has become the popular conclusion that humans were descended from monkeys, and the complex apparatus of Freudian personality analysis become synonymous with the view that the unconscious determines behavior, the equally abstruse argument of *The General Theory* reduced itself to the perception that *the* economic problem was too little demand for goods and services. Casual inspection abundantly demonstrated that there was no shortage of unemployed men and women desperately eager to work for almost any wage higher than zero. Their former employers required only customers to take down the shutters and restart the machines. Farmers grew food and fiber that no one could afford to purchase. The world was not short of potential supply, nor did it lack for customers frustrated by their shortage of cash. Producers were eager to produce, consumers were eager to consume. Separating them was a deficiency of spending power. Effective demand combines thirst for merchandise with the cash to slake it. Hence the Depression lingered because a general deficiency of spending power, of aggregate demand, justified only partial operation of farms and factories.

The total demand for goods and services might or might not justify full employment of facilities and people. It all depended upon the investors. Any purchase of a new machine, any construction of a new factory, any commitment to a new product entails a gamble on the future, an attempt to guess the state of the market two, three, or five years from today. No wonder investment markets are swept by waves of optimism and pessimism, mercurial fluctuations in the "animal spirits" of entrepreneurs who seek to pierce the dark veil of ignorance that shrouds the months and years to come.

Keynes believed that investment incentives were declining. If private investment failed to support aggregate demand at full employment levels, government could and should intervene.

Central bankers might start by offering liberal credit at low rates of interest to business borrowers, but, if such monetary tinkering failed to raise investor expectations of attainable profit, as Keynes predicted, then ready at hand were the more vigorous techniques of fiscal intervention: direct action by government. Franklin Roosevelt's shrewd political instincts made him behave like a Keynesian. Fully instructed politicians might confidently proceed to unbalance the national budget in the course of putting eager men and women to work constructing all manner of needed public works.

To conventional minds, the message was heresy. Deliberate deficits were tantamount to public immorality. To say, with Keynes, that during depressions thrift was no virtue and expenditure no vice was to stand the morality of individual behavior on its head. And to hold government responsible for the performance of an economy was to challenge assumptions as old as Adam Smith that laissez faire was the single, sufficient guide to wholesome economic policy.

Among many politicians and even some economists, the reputation of Keynes is at an all-time low. Whatever the contemporary deficiencies of his theory, Keynesian policy between 1945 and 1973, the year OPEC rearranged the global pecking order, was a howling success. Encouraged by the full employment policies of their governments, investors and consumers in Western Europe and the United States cooperated in a long boom that steadily improved living standards, enlarged welfare protections, and softened class hostility between labor and management. As astute members of the business community came to realize, Keynesian economics, properly domesticated, encouraged lower taxes on corporate profits as stimuli to investment, profitable contracts, succor for faltering corporations, and a wholesome environment for multinational expansion. Political sensitivity to unemployment was perfectly consistent with an apparently endless consumer boom, a feast of profitable marketing.

Within the covers of Keynes's masterpiece, *The General The-*

ory of Employment, Interest and Money, coexisted a radical and a moderate prescription for capitalism. As a radical, Keynes was a secular stagnationist convinced that capitalism's best days were in the past and that investment opportunities were declining. In this mood Keynes favored "somewhat comprehensive socialization of investment" and substantial redistribution of income and wealth in the direction of equality. Mainstream politicians and economists have ignored this aspect of Keynes to this day. Their Keynes is an ally of capitalism and the theorist of growth without end.[5] For them, Keynesian economics in its most conservative guise is reduced to a set of tax and other incentives to investment—the key variable in the determination of Gross National Product and general levels of employment.

American Keynesians in their time of glory were not obsessed with demand, as the ruling caricature now proclaims. During the Kennedy years, Walter Heller and his Council of Economic Advisers colleagues persuaded their intelligent president to endorse a series of encouragements to supply, among them tax credits for new investment, job training designed to improve the skills of the unemployed, and wage-price guidelines addressed to the habit of major corporations and some unions to behave in an inflationary manner.

As with the coincidence of nineteenth century economic progress and laissez-faire ideology, no one can separate coincidence from cause and effect. At the least, the dominance of Keynesian policy did not prevent an outstanding capitalist performance for an entire generation of fortunate Europeans, Japanese, and Americans.

Capitalism is a secular faith. Avarice is a deadly sin as well as the most powerful of economic motives. As that great celebrant of capitalism Joseph Schumpeter regretfully acknowl-

---

[5]In his interesting reappraisal of American policy after World War II, Alan Wolfe argues that growth substituted for, rather than complemented, Keynesian economics. See his *America's Impasse* (Pantheon, 1981).

edged, capitalism strips away the mystery of religion, the glamor of aristocracy, and the awe of monarchy. From the beginning, its most convincing claim has been that it delivers the goods. These are more than the menu of choices in stores and showrooms, and the benefits of the welfare state. They are also validations of cherished aspirations to occupational and financial mobility for parents and children.

Even between 1945 and 1973, there were losers as well as winners. Celebration was muted in southern Italy, Brittany, Scotland, and the north of England. And in our own land, the continuing impact of racial and sexual discrimination registered itself in statistics of comparative income. In all capitalist communities, the distribution of income and wealth remained highly unequal. But on American and European evidence, inequality arouses little popular discontent when it persists within the context of a general improvement in living standards.

III

It is convenient to designate October 1973 as the month the long postwar celebration ground to a halt. OPEC announced its energy revolution and began its redistribution of wealth from oil consumers to oil producers. In the United States, a time of troubles began in the second half of the 1960s. As with OPEC, the phenomenon was political. Between 1964 and 1966, Lyndon Johnson pushed through a complaisant Congress the mass of antipoverty legislation listed under the rubric of the Great Society. A dominant chief executive declared unconditional war against poverty. Unfortunately, he decided to win a shooting war in Vietnam at the same time. Once he had committed himself in mid-1965 to enlarging American operations in Southeast Asia, he should have sought from Congress a huge tax increase to finance—without renewed inflation—a middle-sized war.

Lyndon Johnson dithered. Not without cause, he feared that if he leveled with Congress and the public, appropriations for the Great Society would be slashed and popular support for the war would erode. Therefore, the president rejected his Council of Economic Advisers' advice to raise taxes in January 1966. When, a year later, he did propose a surcharge on personal incomes and corporate profits, Congress haggled over the details for thirteen additional months. By this time, inflation had well and truly taken off.

Because of Vietnam, inflationary pressures began to register themselves in the United States half a decade before OPEC's coup. No mystery surrounded or surrounds those pressures. As both Keynes and ordinary observation suggest, people with more currency stuffed in their fists on the hunt for things to buy, which are increasing in number more slowly than consumer incomes, will create scarcities. Prices will rise. Taking note of this event, unions will bargain for larger wage increases and punctuate their claims with admonitory strikes. As price escalation justifies matching wage boosts, so the latter justify a new round of price hikes. This is the familiar price-wage spiral, easier to initiate than to halt.

One should not exaggerate. When Richard Nixon was inaugurated in January 1969, 5 percent inflation greeted him, a number which in the 1980s would stimulate rejoicing in high places but at the time alarmed a public habituated to virtually stable prices for more than a decade, and worried by the departures from stability of the previous three or four years.

Until the gaudy scandals of Watergate expelled Nixon from the White House, his administration addressed itself internationally to terminating the Vietnam War and domestically to taming inflation without in the process generating serious recession and politically damaging unemployment. Moderately restrained budgetary tactics and mild restraint on credit caused a small recession in 1970 and early 1971. It was a recession that failed to dampen inflation, but it did suffice to make a president concerned about re-election nervous, particularly because some of the opinion polls rated his chances against a popular Democrat like Edmund Muskie as poor. At the start of 1971, accordingly, Mr. Nixon announced that he was a Keynesian, a revelation that stimulated more than one cynic to conclude that Keynes must be obsolete.

The president had larger surprises in reserve. On August 15, 1971, he commandeered all three TV networks to sketch a new strategy. At a stroke, he imposed a 10 percent tariff surcharge on most imports, ended a long-standing policy of buying and selling gold from foreigners at $35 an ounce, and froze most wages and prices for ninety days.[6] The freeze and the ensuing controls period worked reasonably well to restrain inflation and much better as re-election insurance. Because the controls were in place, the Federal Reserve was able to ease credit and the White House to increase spending. The consequent boom was precisely the event needed to swamp the unfortunate George McGovern and install the president in the White House for a second term by a landslide.

Once the election was over, the painful truth emerged that inflation had been suppressed but not eliminated. When controls ended in February 1973, prices spurted upward and by August 1974, when the president was compelled to resign, the American economy was perceived as suffering from a malignant combination of inflation and unemployment, "stagflation" in Paul Samuelson's coinage.

Although Western Europe and Japan imported from OPEC a share of their energy needs larger than that of the United States, OPEC inflicted more inflationary damage on the United

---

[6]The occasion was heavily ironic. In his autobiographical *Six Crises,* Nixon had described with horror the six months he spent as a young compliance attorney in the Office of Price Administration at the start of World War II. Congress had given him standby control authority as a ploy, expecting both that the president would never invoke his new powers and that the Democrats could then blame him for his refusal. The joke was sour also for the president's economic advisers who, with the exception of John Connally, were sturdy opponents of all government interventions into supposedly free markets.

States than on other important oil importers, simply because there was more inflation to feed here than in less disordered economies.[7]

A barrel of oil, which sold in the summer of 1973 for little more than $2, was fetching $36 to $38 by early 1981. In all importing countries except Japan, growth has slowed and unemployment increased. No mystery surrounds these disturbing trends. Compared to the pre-1973 relation between the United States and OPEC, the former pays the latter an extra $90–$100 billion annually. It is a sum very like a tax upon American users, a subtraction from their purchasing power and a transfer of the purchasing power from Americans to foreigners (and domestic energy producers).

Since the uses of oil are pervasive, OPEC's oil revolution has propelled prices upward throughout the economy. Gasoline and home heating oil are significant components of the consumer price index, but petroleum also drives farm equipment, is used in chemical fertilizers, plastics, pharmaceuticals, and synthetic fibers, and shoves upward the parity formulas that govern federal crop supports. OPEC made it more expensive to drive to the supermarket and then compounded the pain by raising the prices of everything in it.

Monetarists who follow in the footsteps of Milton Friedman resemble Isaiah Berlin's hedgehog who knows one big thing. Their big thing is certainty that the only cause of inflation is too much money and the culprit for its creation is the Federal Reserve. Accordingly, the multiplication of the price of even so important a raw material as petroleum cannot duplicate itself in other prices unless the monetary authorities, the seven members of the Board of Governors of the Federal Reserve System,

---

[7]OPEC's multiplication of the price of its elixir had less inflationary effect outside the United States for an additional, more technical reason. OPEC prices oil in dollars. As the value of marks and francs rose and that of the dollar declined, European importers of OPEC oil could trade their own currency for increasing amounts of cheap dollars.

meekly pump up the supply of money and credit by amounts large enough to allow consumers to purchase oil and everything else at higher prices.

If they courageously refrain from such a reaction to inflation, then other prices will diminish because after paying for petroleum products, the public will have less of their income to spend on everything else. After a spell of adjustment, food, clothing, appliances, haircuts, and theater tickets will be cheaper and the cost of living will not be any higher after OPEC's delicate attentions than before.

In an entirely useless way, the monetarists are completely correct. It is indeed true that, in the absence of additional money and credit, a larger proportion of the existing quantity will be devoted to the financing of oil inventories and retail purchases of the stuff. Consumers will have less to spend on other products and services. In time, sellers will get the message and reluctantly slash prices. The critical phrase in the last sentence is *in time*. Perfect competition is an abstraction admired by economists, rarely if ever translated into the real actions of entrepreneurs. In industries like automobiles, dominated by a single producer, or steel, where control is shared by a handful of leading companies, major actors can choose their market strategy whenever sales slacken. They can maintain or even raise prices and accept smaller sales or they can cut prices and sell more cars. In 1974–1975, and again in 1979–1980, the auto industry preferred the first strategy.

Of course even monopolists and oligopolists will ultimately cut prices if sales continue to decline. If the politicians and the bankers wait long enough, shrinking consumer incomes, mounting layoffs, and eroding profits will drive prices down. Along such a path, thousands of efficient manufacturers and retailers will go broke, millions of men and women will lose their jobs, hundreds of billions of dollars of Gross National Product will be forever lost, and the party in office will lose the next election.

I report the obvious. Too much of the American economy

can keep its prices high for many months even when consumer demand registers unwillingness to pay them, to allow any representative government to pursue monetarist tactics indefinitely.[8] So to describe monetarist prospects is not to be misinterpreted as vindication of the Keynesian alternative.

As a practical man, Keynes concentrated his intellectual energies upon mass unemployment rather than inflation. Too blithely, he took it for granted that prices would behave themselves until a society fully employed its labor force and factories. By no particular paradox, the very triumphs of Keynesian demand manipulation after World War II prepared the way for an unhappy sequel.

Generally low rates of unemployment and dependable improvements in wages and other incomes have, for a generation, influenced public expectations. The leaders of great corporations and their stockholders contracted the habit of projecting annual improvement in sales, profits, and dividends. Major unions and large employers agreed on contracts that improved the real incomes of hourly workers. Children expected to drive larger cars and buy bigger houses than their parents could afford.

When the American and other Western economies were growing fairly rapidly, these expectations were realistic. Once growth slows, stops, or turns negative, they cease to be. All the economic performers try frantically to meet their traditional goals. Most of them fail. Ten-percent wage increases are matched with inflation at the same rate or higher. Profits intended for the replacement of old capital equipment are insufficient because of today's unexpectedly inflated prices for new machines.

Bad temper supplants popular optimism about family budg-

---

[8]British governments enjoy five-year terms, unless parliamentary majorities fragment during severe crisis. It remains to be seen whether Mrs. Thatcher, a determined monetarist, will persevere in a policy which by the summer of 1981 had propelled unemployment to 12.4 percent, by far the worst figure since the 1930s.

ets. Endless pursuit of prices by wages and wages by prices actually worsens the situation of average families, pushed into steeper marginal tax brackets by higher take-home pay that can be traded for diminishing amounts of merchandise. In the terminology of game theory, all the income claimants play a zero-sum game, one in which the gains of some match themselves against the losses of others, much as in a convivial poker game the algebraic sum of winnings and losings always equals zero at evening's end.

The politics are nasty. More Social Security for the elderly is financed by higher payroll taxes inflicted upon their children and grandchildren. If women and minorities are promoted, white males are not. Special programs for young workers adversely affect their parents. Successful politics in democracies requires general distribution of good things to as many groups and localities as possible. The 1950s and the 1960s were an excellent period in which to be an officeholder.

The 1970s and the 1980s are dangerous times for presidents and smaller fry. A great many of his former associates have ardently testified to Jimmy Carter's incompetence, but the man was at least as unlucky as he was inept. It was his fate to become president at the end of a long boom. Woe to any political party so trapped by fate. The economic growth that had financed the Great Society was a phenomenon of the past. Carter's constituents, resistant to this unpleasing reality, expected their president to keep his promises—less inflation, more jobs, universal health care, larger pensions, welfare reform, and cheaper energy. No president worked and prayed harder to succeed. Failure was almost inevitable.

OPEC was by no means the only reason why the American economy sputtered to a near halt. In the 1970s a large assortment of overdue bills came due. One set was environmental. Throughout American history, businessmen, farmers, and developers had treated land, water, and atmosphere as free goods, inexhaustible resources to be exploited for personal gain. Mining firms devastated mountain landscapes. Paper, steel, and copper mills dumped noxious chemicals into handy streams and fouled the atmosphere with particulate wastes from coal and oil high in sulphur. Employers treated human beings almost as casually. Little attention and fewer resources were devoted to health and safety in factories and mines. With fine impartiality, producers neglected to the considerable extent they dared the safety, wholesomeness, and reliability of the products they sold to their customers.

In elevated economic terminology, I have listed a series of externalities—costs of production shifted to workers, consumers, and the communities in which they reside. Coal miners disabled by emphysema or black lung disease became financial charges upon their families, union, or publicly financed hospitals. Sufferers from brown lung ailments contracted in textile mills shared their experience. Communities in search of clean water built purification plants out of the proceeds of taxes. The best that an individual damaged by an unsafe product could do was find a negligence lawyer to sue the offending producer.

At some date, public reaction against such abuses was certain to generate political response. Occupational health and safety are working-class issues, but clean air and water, safe autos and appliances, reliable prescription drugs, and processed foods free of carcinogens, touch the vital interests of the middle class as much as those of fellow citizens who are either richer or poorer.

Popular indignation was overdue and its scale was on the whole more temperate than the misdemeanors and felonies which had prompted the emotion. To say so is not to deny that the grudging compliance of corporate America to new health and safety, environmental, and product quality standards cost money, and required diversion of funds available for new plant and equipment to the purchase instead of smokestack scrubbers, safety devices, water treatment units, and allied capital goods. According to the strange canons of national income measurement, cleaner air and water and safer products and working environments do not count as part of the Gross National Product. There is consequently no statistical offset to the diversion of investment resources required to achieve these ends.

To his personal credit, and at great political cost, Jimmy Carter tried his futile best to alert his discontented constituents to the narrowing of the economic horizons. With fatal lack of eloquence, he preached conservation. In fumbling fashion, he aimed at an acceptable consensus about resource use and income distribution. Alfred Kahn, powerless enforcer of the administration's wage and price standards for noninflationary behavior, wryly commented that his own major accomplishment in office was growth of a moustache.

The responses politically available are few. A community may come to agreement about fair shares for labor and capital, men and women, old and young, farmers and consumers, declining and rising communities. Resisting the necessity for such a social compact, the voters may elect a president who agrees with them and pledges himself to restore a land of boundless abundance and enormous opportunity: in two words, Ronald Reagan. They are likely to discover that their temporary hero will do no better than his vanquished adversary, but that the issue of distribution of limited national resources and output will be settled in ways neither anticipated nor desired.

IV

Ronald Reagan, like many of his predecessors, claims no originality of thought. His new philosophy of wealth, the ideological garment of naked avarice, is the joint product of names unfamiliar to the public until just yesterday. Stockman? Kemp? Laffer? Wanniski? Gilder? Aside from their friends and family, who, a season ago, would have identified them as movers and shakers of national policy, familiar figures in the corridors of power, authors of best-selling polemics, and sufficient causes for alarm on the part of the poor, aged, handicapped, female, black, Hispanic, and urban?

The new heroes are young, fervent, dogmatic, and, in several instances, converts to their current vision. Among mainstream social scientists of conventionally liberal *or* conservative stripe, their guild credentials are shaky and their solutions too simple to please specialists. To the lay person, this description may read much like a recommendation. The economic guild has had little to celebrate in recent years. It may be time for outsiders to have their chance.

Consider first the inspiring career of David A. Stockman, risen, as the world knows, to the glory of director of the Office of Management and Budget. In his mid-thirties, this stripling, according to his journalistic admirer, *Time*'s Hugh Sidey, "may be the greatest repository of information on the U. S. government now in Washington." In time past a vigorous opponent of the Vietnam War and organizer of Vietnam Summer demonstrations against American involvement, Stockman migrated from Michigan to Washington as an aide to then Congressman John Anderson, equipped with a recommendation from Daniel Patrick Moynihan with whom he had studied at Harvard's John F. Kennedy School. By 1976, he was ready to seek and win election to Congress from his native Michigan as a conservative Republican. In Congress, he stood out among his colleagues because of unremitting zeal for budget-cutting and a facility, rare among politicians, with computers. As Hugh Sidey admiringly added, "With the help of a handful of aides, he analyzed every significant governmental issue." Oh, wow, as Charles Reich used to say.

On February 18, 1981, this veteran of a mere four years in the House of Representatives, an infant among grizzled elders, presented his former colleagues with the Stockman "black book," a massive document entitled *America's New Beginning: A Program for Economic Recovery.* Seldom in any presidential administration has an individual so clearly imposed the stamp of his own convictions on national policy. The details will be supplied later. Suffice it here to say that translation of this scheme into legislative fact approximates slaughter of most of the Great Society, reversal of faltering recent progress in the general direction of racial and sexual equality, acceleration of economic decline in the Northeast and Midwest, unneeded stimulation of the booming Sun Belt economy, redistribution of income from poor to rich, much diminished worker protection against accident and hazardous chemicals, erosion of unemployment compensation, enlargement of low-wage markets, and weakened environmental protection.

Not at all a bad day's work for a pleasant chap equipped "with the mod-cut mop of hair, engaging smile and soft voice" celebrated by the media.[9]

Alas, the media magnates who puff up political personalities take equal delight in deflating them. As the world came to know in November 1981 after the publication of William Greider's "The Education of David Stockman" in the *Atlantic Monthly*, as early as the second month of the Reagan era our hero was busily cooking the budget projections to White House taste. By spring, he had soured on supply-side economics. By summer, his private conversations with journalists and a few politicians contrasted sharply with his vigorous advocacy of the administration program in congressional testimony and on the Sunday talk shows.

No wonder Mr. Reagan angrily summoned his fair-haired boy emeritus to the Oval Office for a dressing down. For old-movie freaks, that painful luncheon inevitably recalled those venerable Andy Hardy flicks in which a stern Judge Hardy (Lewis Stone) confronted his errant son, Andy (Mickey Rooney), and administered severe, character-building punishment. Few can be better qualified than the president to revive the Judge Hardy role. For his part, Stockman at his contrite press conference demonstrated considerable aptitude for the juvenile lead. Indeed our David's rapid transitions from anti-war activism to divinity studies to Moynihan neoconservatism to supply-side economics to the budget-balancing priorities of Republican graybeards usually are indulged as privileges of the

---

[9]The quoted words, all written by Hugh Sidey, appeared in *Time*, May 18, 1981, p. 23.

young. Stockman may yet enroll in the Democratic Socialist Organizing Committee.

The grade B film echoes aside, Greider and Stockman make a pair of important contributions to contemporary political history. Greider documents the rapidity with which a highly intelligent public official came to understand the deficiencies of supply-side doctrine. Greider also demonstrates how accurate the critics of the new revelation have been in their denunciations of tax and spending cuts. Skeptics questioned from the outset both the equity and the workability of Reagan policies. Stockman's negative answers on both scores powerfully buttress the opposition cause.

Reagonomics will never be the same again. For this happy event, we must thank the enterprising Greider and the indiscreet, selectively candid Stockman.

Enough for the moment of our tarnished Saint George. He fares well against the budget dragons, if less well with his president. His great friend (at least prior to that fatal December) and congressional ally Jack Kemp is somewhat older and more experienced. Born in 1935 in Los Angeles, Kemp played quarterback for thirteen years on the Buffalo Bills successfully enough to make all-pro in his best seasons. As his reflexes slowed, he drifted into politics like many other professional sports stars, astronauts, and released prisoners of war. Since 1970, he has represented a blue-collar district in Congress. Russell Baker's Great Mentioner from time to time drops his name as a gubernatorial, senatorial, even presidential possibility.

Kemp's political reputation began to change when he encountered Jude Wanniski, former *Wall Street Journal* editorialist, convert to economic revelation according to Arthur Laffer, and zealot with an engaging sense of fun. For Kemp, and probably for the United States, the meeting had momentous consequences. Congress is notoriously stuffed with conservatives in both major parties, invariably predisposed to save the Republic from the fate of the Roman Empire by cutting taxes and limiting social spending. To distinguish oneself against the competition, a legislator requires both extraordinary enthusiasm and a favorite nostrum.

A book doesn't hurt. As for the enthusiasm, Kemp, a booster to the core, displayed the arts of salesmanship expected of an active Jaycee and Outstanding Young Man. His *American Renaissance,* the book he wrote with the acknowledged help of Wanniski, is a splendid example of positive thought. Here is a fair sample: "This is a book about the American renaissance, about the revival—already under way—of a strong, prosperous, proud America. And so this is a book of optimism, of hope, of national renewal. In a phrase, this is a book about the American dream, that amalgam of promise and effort and desire that make this country the hope of civilized people everywhere."

Why, recently, has that dream been slipping away? Listen: "If we only stop what we have been doing to destroy ourselves by destroying incentives, we can once again thrive." As we deserve to thrive of course: *"We are the most free and most educated, talented, energetic, and healthy people on earth—and we are now operating at less than half our potential, perhaps less than a third our potential!"* (Kemp's emphasis all the way.) Our teeth are brightest and our laundry whitest.

You guessed right. The villain who bars us from our birthright is government: "There's no telling what we can accomplish if only the government would get out of the way and let us load the wagon." Americans are in luck. There is nothing complicated about the taming of government and ensuing release of national energies. A person need do no more than comprehend the connection between taxes and incentives to work, save, and invest. And the key to enlightenment is the Laffer curve. As summarized by Kemp, its essence need not elude the meanest intellect: "At some point, additional taxes so discourage the activity being taxed, such as working or investing, that they yield less revenue rather than more. There are, after all, two rates that yield the same amount of revenue: high tax rates on low production, or low rates on high production. . . . There is . . . some rate that allows the government maximum revenue and yet does not discourage maximum production." Back in the eighteenth century the wise Scot David Hume anticipated Arthur Laffer in these 1756 words of sooth: "Exorbitant taxes, like extreme necessity, destroy industry by producing despair; and even before they reach this pitch, they raise the wages of the labourer and manufacturer, and heighten the price of all commodities. An attentive disinterested legislature will observe the point when the emolument ceases and the prejudice begins."[10]

A niggling critic at this juncture might ask how a "disinterested" politician, a creature encountered as frequently as a strolling unicorn, locates tax rates threatening to productive activity and menacing to treasury revenue. Faith helps mightily. It must have been faith that taxes already were dangerously high that induced Kemp and his Senate colleague Delaware's William Roth to sponsor a three-year program of successive 10 percent cuts in personal income levies. Ronald Reagan's endorsement of Kemp-Roth while a candidate and then as president transformed Jack Kemp into a major political figure, the third ranking member of the Republican House leadership hierarchy.[11]

Will tax cuts really induce consumers to spend less and save more? Will parallel reductions in business tax liabilities promote an investment boom? Will the rebound in growth rates so induced more than restore temporary losses in tax receipts? Isn't the danger real that more inflation instead of more growth will be generated?

Overlooked by supply-siders are such odd phenomena in the capitalist world as the British combination of extremely generous incentives to investment and dangerously low levels of investment, the German combination of generous social ben-

---

[10]David Hume, *Writings on Economics,* ed. Eugene Rotwein (Edinburgh: Thomas Nelson & Sons, 1955), p. 87.
[11]The quotations all come from *An American Renaissance* (New York: Basic Books, 1979), pp. I, II, 51, 100.

efits, high investment, and, until the last year or two, economic growth at rates substantially higher than those registered in this country, and the Japanese reconciliation of cozy collaboration between government and major producers with a competitive élan that has terrified Western European and American rivals. No contemporary example is available of rapid growth in an economy organized according to the liking of our supply-siders.

Supply-siders testily dismiss Keynesian apprehensions that Americans will react in customary ways to slightly larger paychecks. Trained from infancy to spend even faster than they earn, consumers have been in the habit of disbursing 95 cents out of any additional dollar that flows their way and saving a mere nickel to revitalize the American economy. Most economists even of monetarist persuasion are inclined to anticipate only modest additions to savings from Kemp-Roth. In the supply-side view, they are dead wrong to assume "that every firm and every household will continue behaving in exactly the same way before the imposition of the tax reform as they would after the tax change. Therefore, when Congress is presented information about the likely effects of tax policies . . . the deck is stacked against proposals which temporarily decrease tax revenues but stimulate the long-term growth of the economy."[12]

In the opening year of the Reagan era, the cold-hearted, sharp-minded folks who trade in stocks and bonds for their living on Wall Street gave daily evidence of skepticism about supply-side economics. If, as expert opinion holds true, rising bond prices register confidence that in the long run inflation and interest rates will subside, then sluggish or actually declining bond markets inevitably testify to the opposite opinion. Low bond prices, high yields on old securities, and similar interest

---

[12]The words are those of Michael Boskin, a conservative Stanford economist, cited by Kemp, p. 100.

rates attached to new issues, tell a tale disappointing to the prophets of the new economic order. Investment types will vote Republican. They will contribute generously to their candidate's presidential campaign funds. However, they will not buy bonds when their professional analysis instructs them to sell bonds. It was quite enough to sour the president's sunny disposition and impel him to comment that Wall Street was a bad source of economic advice, inhabited by types guilty of examining the universe through a "narrow glass."

Reaganauts are lavish users of faith, frequently of a secular variety, as in their touching, conceivably autobiographical, confidence in the propulsive force of avarice. On occasion, as in the person of Interior Secretary James Watt, faith is aggressively fundamentalist Christian. At his confirmation hearing, Mr. Watt casually confided to the senators in attendance that "I do not know how many future generations we can count on before the Lord returns." Otherwise rare in the secretary's utterances, this uncertainty appeared, mysteriously to justify opening of public lands to coal miners, oil explorers, lumbermen, resort developers, stock grazers, and other predators. Scripture, asserted Mr. Watt, endorsed his plan: "My responsibility is to follow the Scriptures which call upon us to occupy the land until Jesus returns."[13]

On points of faith and morals, no supply-sider can speak with more of the special grace accorded the authors of best-sellers than George Gilder, perpetrator of *Wealth and Poverty,* a volume displayed on national television by the president himself. It is a manifesto to infidels, glowingly celebrated by David Stockman as "Promethean in its intellectual power and insight," Jack Kemp who testified that "With an eloquent style, George Gilder gives us the first book in years that compellingly makes the case for the moral as well as the practical merits of capitalism," and Harvard's neoconservative sociologist Nathan

---

[13] See the *Washington Post,* May 24, 1981, p. L 5.

Glazer who just had to admit that "George Gilder's *Wealth and Poverty* is a really remarkable analysis of American social and economic policy that demolishes a host of pieties as to the causes of poverty and the conditions that overcome it."[14]

I happen to know George Gilder as an amiable soul prey to convulsions of enthusiasm that are transformed into entire books. Like his friend David Stockman, he did not always believe in the truths he now holds precious. In the wake of the 1964 Goldwater debacle, the young Gilder, at the time a liberal Republican of the Ivy League, Ripon Society totem, published in *The Party That Lost Its Head* a scathing blast at extremism and an indulgent defense of the welfare state.

As the boy grew older, he fell into bad company. From a gaggle of intellectually and politically reactionary social scientists, he extracted an extreme version of antifeminism. God, it seems, has implanted in male genes drives to hunt and dominate and in female DNA complementary yearnings to nurture husbands and progeny. Evidently women who insist on competing for good jobs with male rivals, and, worse still, seek authority over men, thwart their own natures and mortally wound male egos.

Such logic lays bare the diseases of welfare. Its very existence encourages men, especially black men, to live off the benefits collected by women, instead of seeking jobs to support their mates. It follows that for the good of welfare families themselves, these subsidies to male misbehavior and treachery to masculine nature must be reduced if not eliminated. Let the idle males hunt and forage like the rest of us.

Like his endorsers, Gilder is fascinated by the Laffer curve. But he applies a highly original spiritual patina to the connection between incentives and marginal tax rates central to Laffer

---

[14] I culled these tributes from the dust cover of the Basic Books (1981) hardcover edition. They attest to the smooth operation of the "new boy" network of supply-siders. Political and literary coteries have from the dawn of literacy played the game of scratching each other's backs: You praise my book, I'll take care to praise yours. The newcomers should be congratulated for catching on so quickly.

policy prescriptions. Gilder considers the traditional defense of capitalism inadequate. Mere efficiency in the output of goods and services, gratification of human desires for material things, ultimately offends our spiritual nature. Capitalism's reason for survival, its justification as a set of social and political as well as economic relations, must be its appeal to motives higher than mere greed, and activities less humdrum than buying low and selling high.

Seek and ye shall find. Gilder's hunt for the spiritual within capitalism carries him toward investment behavior. Does not an investor make a leap of faith whenever he gambles on the future profitability of a new product, machine, factory, office building, or residential subdivision? Is not his act akin to the communal charity of Pacific chieftains who treated their neighbors and dependents to lavish potlatches without the least assurance of reciprocity? Like the islanders of Oceania, in the dawn of anthropological time even before Margaret Mead invented Samoa, our own capitalists know in their hearts that "Capitalism begins with giving." For, "Capitalist production entails faith—in one's neighbors, in one's society, and in the compensatory logic of the cosmos. Search and you shall find, give and you will be given unto, supply creates its own demand." God is a capitalist and the world is created in His image: "Under capitalism, the ventures of reason are launched into a world ruled by morality and Providence. The gifts will succeed only to the extent that they are altruistic and spring from an understanding of others. They depend on faith in an essentially fair and responsive humanity. In such a world, one can give without a contract of compensation. One can venture without the assurance of reward. One can seek the surprises of profit, rather than the more limited benefits of contractual pay. One can take the initiative amid radical perils and uncertainties." To sum it all up: "The ultimate strength and crucial weakness of both capitalism and democracy are their reliance on individual creativity and courage, leadership and morality,

intuition and faith. But there is no alternative, except medioc-
rity."[15] We obviously need to revise our opinions of the found-
ing Robber Barons and their contemporary descendants. These
were men of faith.

Supply-siders, then, represent a new strain among conserva-
tives. Such good, gray Republican wheelhorses as Arthur F.
Burns, who served Dwight Eisenhower as Council of Economic
Advisers chairman, served Richard Nixon as Federal Reserve
chairman, and now serves Ronald Reagan as ambassador to the
Federal Republic of Germany; Paul McCracken and Herbert
Stein, Richard Nixon's Council of Economic Advisers chairman; and Alan Greenspan, occupant of the position during the
Ford interregnum, are conspicuously deficient in mysticism.
They also lack faith in Kemp-Roth tax magic. It is far from
certain that they understand "the compensatory logic of the
cosmos." One doubts that they share Gilder's confidence in "an
essentially fair and responsive humanity." Burns and company
share cravings for balanced budgets, followed by lower taxes,
and smaller government.

Old-fashioned conservatives and ascendant supply-siders diverge over the timing of tax cuts. The former expect them to
add more to inflation than to saving and investment. As we
have seen, the latter anticipate the sort of surge in saving and
investment that in short order accelerates growth and restores
briefly lost Treasury tax receipts. Supply-siders believe that the
United States is already poised on the Laffer curve at a point
that recalls David Hume's apprehension about "exorbitant
taxes" and their propensity to encourage rather than check
inflation.

Economists, Keynesian, monetarist, or eclectic, are a gloomy
lot. Supply-siders are refreshingly enthusiastic, optimistic, and
self-confident. *An American Renaissance, The Way the World
Works,* and *Wealth and Poverty*: these are titles selected by men
who recognize the superhighway to revival, know the mech-

---

[15]The quotations from *Wealth and Poverty* are on pp. 21, 24, and 27.

anisms of global economics, and tend the springs of affluence. As in the past,[16] these newcomers are either self-instructed amateurs or professionals strayed from orthodoxy. Noneconomists to a pundit, Kemp, Gilder, and Stockman have paid their respects to their instructors: Arthur Laffer and two gifted intellectual journalists, Irving Kristol and Jude Wanniski. Little claim is made for intellectual originality. On the contrary, supply-siders proudly wear the banner of classical economics. They have restated the truths they found there with admirable energy and an almost touching naïveté about the institutional realities of late capitalism. Ours is a time in which enormous enterprises like Du Pont swallow equally huge corporate giants like Conoco, number nine in the energy list. The merged companies will rank in size just below the Ford Motor Company. Du Pont will pay Conoco's stockholders a cool $7.3 billion. The fierce enforcer of the antitrust laws, Attorney General William French Smith, reassures all parties that bigness is not necessarily either unlawful or inefficient. What on earth does an entity with combined sales of $32.4 billion possess in common with the competitive markets of classical theory, in which hosts of buyers confront numerous smaller sellers, avidly cutting each other's prices? Advanced economies are dominated by large institutions that prefer merger and collusion to competition. The people who decide their investment policies are members of committees disinclined to "give without a contract of compensation" or "take the initiative amid radical perils and uncertainties."

Enterprises and industries in trouble routinely shuttle to Washington in pursuit of loan guarantees, quotas, trigger-price mechanisms, and similar shelters from the icy blast of competition from Japanese, European, and Third World rivals. At home, it is the trucking industry and the Teamsters Union, not

---

[16]Adam Smith was a moral philosopher, David Ricardo a retired stockbroker and arbitrageur, and John Stuart Mill a logician and student of government. His colleagues considered Keynes dangerously heterodox long before *The General Theory*.

unrepentant Keynesians, who oppose deregulation. It is the airlines who regret their earlier endorsement of deregulation. Faith ignores mountains more easily than it moves them. For supply-siders faced with evidence that competitive élan has flagged, a response is readily available. The government has been at it again. Just as misguided public benevolence has damaged the character of families on welfare, congressional and presidential responsiveness to the pleas of frantic businessmen has dampened the self-reliance of executives and investors.

Better days are ahead. Lighten the heavy burdens of government upon individual initiative. Still the meddling hand of the bureaucrat. Set our capitalists free. They cannot enrich themselves without enriching the rest of us.

2

taxes: the falwell fix

Material wealth is God's
way of blessing people who
put Him first.

REVEREND JERRY FALWELL

The tax code sensitively registers the relative strength of interest groups. With such rare aberrations as its adoption of a
windfall tax on oil profits, Congress and presidents have habitually coddled the energy industry in salute to its political power
and role as a source of campaign funds. Exemption from taxation of interest payments subsidizes home builders and home
owners, as well as industries like autos that market their products by installment sales.

In a variety of ways, Congress has mitigated apparently high
rates of taxation on personal incomes. It is relatively easy for
the affluent to arrange to receive significant fractions of income
as capital gains subject to much lower rates of taxation than
wages and salaries. Income can be sheltered in individual retirement accounts. Doctors and lawyers can reap significant tax
relief by incorporating. Broadly speaking, the tax system operates most harshly against ordinary wage and salary earners,

who are unable to warm themselves in tax shelters, deduct personal consumption as business expenses, or benefit from the indulgent handling of income from property. Tax policy is social policy. Washington shaped the tax code after World War II to favor the growth of suburbs. Congress complemented mortgage interest and local property tax deductibility with Federal Housing Administration guarantees of mortgages and a huge network of interstate highways, the major domestic initiative of the Eisenhower administration. To favor suburbs is to damage the cities from which a generation of home owners moved. Renters cannot subtract the fraction of rent that represents taxes. The federal government until very recently gave their buses and subways no help.

Tax policy is also racial politics. New suburbanites in the post-World War II generation were overwhelmingly white. The migrants from the South and Puerto Rico who replaced them were darker in skin tone. For much of this period, FHA reluctance to extend its mortgage guarantees to "changing neighborhoods," the usual euphemism for sections of cities in which departing whites saluted arriving blacks, accelerated the deterioration of inner cities.

These are the realities. However, there are decencies to be observed. Presidents and legislators rarely state frankly their intentions to reward the corporate interests who financed their campaigns nor do they often play on the prejudices of their constituents. Their game is played another way.

Taxes are always too high. Hence in democracies, statesmen on safari for revenue they can safely extract from resentful constituents tend to rely upon high principle. By turns, they justify any alteration of tax policy as equitable or efficient. The second adjective implies that a good tax stimulates productive work and investment.

What is fair? Should the poor pay more? If the rich shoulder heavier tax burdens, how can tax collectors justify hurting God's chosen children?

The traditional argument for progressive taxation is utilitarian. As Jeremy Bentham expressed that argument in the nineteenth century, human beings were assumed to be, much as in Adam Smith's *Wealth of Nations,* rational, self-centered, and hedonistic—seekers after pleasure and avoiders of pain. Our capacity as receptacles of pleasure is finite. Pleasure diminishes, Bentham argued, as the quantity of any pleasing item in our possession increases. Second portions are consumed more slowly and yield less gratification than initial servings. As with food, so also with TVs, oriental carpets, European travel, fast cars, and pleasure boats. The rule or generalization applies to the most comprehensive of all sources of joy, money itself.[1] To a family clinging to the poverty line, an extra $100 causes celebration. For the really rich, that $100 will be noted only by accountants indentured to their service.

For tax policy, this version of *Homo oeconomicus* conveys momentous implications. Because money conveys less pleasure as it piles up in the hands of any individual, it follows that the affluent should suffer less from a 20 percent tax on income than those less financially well endowed. The citizen earning $20,000 will suffer more acutely after the subtraction of $4,000 than the chap required to fork over $40,000 out of a $200,000 income. Or so the theory goes. In tax matters, strict justice requires that all victims feel equally mulcted after the Internal Revenue Service has done its worst. The golden rule of the tax tables demands collection of a larger *fraction* of taxable income as income rises.

So far, possibly so easy. From here onward, the going becomes trickier. How much larger ought that fraction be? How can the wisest of legislators peer within human skulls and measure the agitation of quivering nerve endings? Testimony from the victims is unreliable, for the self-interest of each taxpayer will induce exaggeration of his own misery. The best that might be said with some assurance is that both learned theory

---

[1] In economic jargon, this is a statement of the principle of diminishing marginal utility of money. Each extra dollar confers less utility than its predecessor.

and public sentiment argue for an element of progression some-
where in the tax structure.

Specialists term the progression thus far discussed, "verti-
cal." As taxable income rises, the rate applicable to extra bits
also increases and so consequently must the average rate of
assessment. Tax justice, however, is incomplete unless revenue
collectors treat similarly circumstanced individuals or families
in the same way. This stipulation bears the label "horizontal
equity." It is easier stated than codified. Are large families and
small ones, old and young, renters and home owners, farmers
and city dwellers, healthy and infirm, the salaried and the collectors of dividends, and residents of sunny states and shiverers
in cold ones, truly "similarly circumstanced"? No, no, and
again no, vociferate the Senate Finance Committee and the
House Ways and Means Committee. Allowable deductions for
medical expenses, mortgage interest and property taxes, attest
to public endorsement of indulgence to the ill and to home
owners. Capital gains are a variety of property income taxed
more lightly than other returns from ownership because, pre-
sumably, greater risk of loss and greater uncertainty of profit
are attached to sales of securities and real property.

Tax reformers have long devoted themselves to increasing
progression in personal income tax schedules and closing loopholes through which adroit taxpayers wriggle. When Jimmy
Carter tried his hand at tax reform, he frequently decried the
unfairness of permitting high living businessmen to deduct as
expenses their three-martini lunches, but prohibiting the honest
working man from doing the same with his plebeian bologna
sandwich and can of Schlitz. Although it is asserted on excellent authority that, these days, serious negotiation is conducted
over Perrier water with a thin slice of lemon on the side, the
consumers of business meals predictably cried foul. But a good
many cold-cut consumers also objected to the subversive notion
of compelling the business community to finance its own enter-
tainment and perks. A coalition of restaurant, hotel, theater,

and sporting event operators, and their employees mobilized in self-defense of profits and jobs. When the subsidized luxuries of the prosperous furnish income for the poor and respectable, who is left to cry for justice? On contemporary evidence, tax reform is another faded liberal passion, to adapt Richard Hofstadter's apt verdict upon the antitrust movement. Even if equity were more popular, the decisive protection of the wealthy is the eye-glazing complexity of the tax code. Only skilled professionals at the service of large corporations and affluent individuals begin to comprehend that code.

At best, equity must compete and occasionally clash with concern for economic efficiency, and the impact upon incentives to work, save, and invest. The tax reformer's loopholes are the special interest lobbyist's valuable incentives to productive effort, capital formation, energy independence, successful rivalry with the Japanese, better housing for middle America, and entrepreneurial optimism. Punitive taxation, it is only common sense to realize, diminishes any activity to which it is applied. Tax corporate profits and dividends too severely and investors will cease to buy new issues of stocks and bonds. Their behavior will deprive corporate America of funds needed to replace elderly machines and construct new factories. Tax additional income from work at steep marginal rates and people will go to the beach on a sunny Saturday instead of doing their bit to revitalize America by putting in some overtime.

Once again, this connection between taxes and incentives is much easier to assert than it is to translate into detailed policy. For one thing, the sparse empirical evidence available is contradictory and thus not completely supportive of intuition. A few studies tentatively conclude that as marginal tax rates decline, members of the labor force prefer to take most of their benefits in added leisure instead of more income. That is to say, they work fewer hours for the same after-tax reward. Also available are studies that tend in the opposite direction and suggest that lower marginal tax rates will indeed evoke more work effort and greater investor enthusiasm.

It is permissible to be skeptical about extravagant claims for the incentive impact of lower marginal tax rates on a second ground, embarrassing to supply-side enthusiasts if they did not generally ignore it. Broadly speaking, taxes on capital gains, large incomes, and corporate profits have been steadily declining for a dozen years. For practical purposes, Congress has been quietly phasing out the corporate profits tax as a revenue source. Any corporate executive worthy of his spurs negotiates the sort of contract with his employer that confers substantial sums upon him completely sheltered from tax.[2] Why, it might legitimately be asked, haven't these amply rewarded managers and investors already unleashed the investment boom needed to renew economic growth and make America great again?

As will shortly emerge, inflation and rising taxes on payrolls have afflicted Americans earning low and average incomes. Their financial superiors in the executive and investing class have kept well ahead of inflation and tax collectors.

II

We have returned to Reagan country where the landscape seems quite different from the one just viewed. Representative of the administration's perspective is this economist's summing up of domestic troubles:

> The United States economy has veered off course, and much of this malfunction can be traced to manmade disincentives to produce income and wealth and to allocate resources efficiently. There is also a clear consensus that our major economic goal for

---

[2] When interest rates are high, corporations frequently lend large sums to favored employees at 4 to 6 percent interest rates.

the 1980s must be to restore healthy noninflationary economic growth and that this can only be accomplished in an environment with a more stable, predictable, and lower rate of monetary expansion, a slower rate of growth in government spending, and a concerted effort to remove disincentives that obstruct working, saving, investing, and innovating.[3]

Now and forevermore, taxes are disincentives. Diminish them and America will bloom.

In its original form, the White House urged a "clean" tax bill upon Congress—Kemp-Roth plus matching boons to business. Congress, bless its generous heart, accepted the Kemp-Roth principle[4] and attendant alleviation of corporate tax burdens and added some bounties of its own, among them immediate reduction of the top 70 percent rate on property income to 50 percent, partial repeal of windfall profits levies on oil revenue, and amendment of inheritance tax provisions which all but repeal efforts to limit the transmission of large estates from generation to generation.[5] As enacted, Kemp-Roth cuts personal income taxes by percentages of 5, 10, and 10, the first time Congress has tipped its hand for so long a period.

The alteration in the tax treatment of business is slightly more technical. It focuses upon depreciation. Depreciation, a deductible cost, is an allowance for the decline in useful life of machines and structures with the passage of time. The more substantial that allowance is in any given tax period, the smaller consequently is the percentage of earnings subject to the corpo-

---

[3]The wisdom emanates from Michael J. Boskin in *The Economy in the 1980s,* a 1980 publication which originated at the Institute for Contemporary Studies, one of many conservative "think tanks" that deface the California coast.

[4]President Reagan compromised on the size and timing of first-year reductions in levies on personal incomes. As a result, the 1981 cut was only 5 percent (for the entire year) and began October 1, instead of July 1.

[5]The first $600,000 of any estate will henceforth be exempt from tax, a presumed benefit to family farmers and small business operators. A husband can protect his spouse in her years of mourning by deeding his entire estate to her; however large that estate happens to be, it will be utterly untaxed.

rate profit tax. Moreover, the sooner equipment and structures can be fully depreciated, the more quickly can funds be made available to replace worn-out capital items with technologically superior devices.

Let us cast a calm eye on the two major parts of Reagan tax therapy, beginning with Kemp-Roth. Superficially, what could be fairer than reductions in their tax liabilities by the same percentage for every taxpayer? Naturally those who earn the most will enjoy the fattest tax savings, but these are the very people who paid large taxes to begin with.

It is not that simple, unfortunately. Taxes never are. Nor are the consequences of Kemp-Roth as equitable as its proponents assert them to be. Whether an individual or a family comes out better or worse off at the conclusion of three years of Kemp-Roth depends upon the impact of bracket creep and Social Security payroll deductions upon his after-tax income. Before the 1981 tax revolution, the lowest rate applicable to earned income between $3,400 and $5,500 for married couples was 14 percent. The top rate of 70 percent used to be applied to income in excess of $215,400 *if* any portion of such pleasing sums was derived from dividends, rent, or other income from property. The largest of incomes, if derived entirely from salary, was subject to a maximum levy of 50 percent.

Between humble folk in the 14 percent bracket and swells in the 50 to 70 percent bracket are the vast majority of taxpayers whose income is assessed at a series of rising rates in successively higher tax brackets. To say carelessly that a boost in salary throws its recipient into a higher bracket is not equivalent to the general misinterpretation that an individual's entire taxable income is now subject to a higher rate. The higher or marginal rate applies only to the last increment of income, the salary boost. However, the *average* rate paid on income subject to tax naturally moves upward every time a different, higher rate is imposed on a portion of the taxable total. If an individual pays 14 percent on an initial $2,000 of taxable income, 16 percent on the next $2,000, and 18 percent on still a third $2,000, the *average* rate paid is 16 percent. A salary increase that propels this person into the 20 percent bracket raises the average rate to 17 percent.

Inflation creep, as pervasive as it is excoriated, is, notoriously, one of the effects of inflation, in addition to slowed growth in real income. In the last decade, few wage earners have experienced improvements in their wages which matched, let alone exceeded, the inexorable upward march of the consumer price index. Before the 1981 tax reductions came into effect, a family of four who in 1980 earned $15,000 paid $1,242, or 8.3 percent in federal income tax. If, between 1980 and 1984, inflation averaged 9.2 percent, the family's income in 1984 had to expand to $21,390 merely to stay even.

However, the family stayed even only *before* tax, for on an income of $21,390, at 1980 tax rates, it enjoyed the dubious privilege of surrendering to IRS $2,387 or 11.2 percent of its inflation-swollen income. Bracket creep inflicts upon this family a tax increase of $616 or 26 percent. Inflation and the progression in the personal income tax structure combine to worsen the financial situation of families who can do no better than match wage increases to the escalation of the consumer price index. In declining industries and regions, most workers do worse. Their real earnings deteriorate before tax and still more after tax.

Bad enough. There is worse to come. For large numbers of Americans of low and moderate income, Social Security deductions from their paychecks are heavier burdens than levies on personal income. On January 1, 1981, the Social Security payroll tax rate rose from 6.13 percent to 6.65 percent and maximum earnings subject to the new rate increased from $25,900 to $29,700. For earnings of $15,000 the consequence was a 0.5 percent hike in tax liability, for earnings of $30,000 an increase of 0.8 percent, but for $100,000 heavy hitters a mere 0.2 percent. And the $100,000 family that escapes tax liability on $70,000 of its income from work almost surely supplements earnings with property income completely free from Social Security tax assessment.

The best to be said on behalf of Kemp-Roth is that in its absence most Americans with incomes below $30,000 would fare even worse. Nevertheless, the apparent fairness of across-the-board tax reduction dissolves once account is taken as well of bracket creep and the financing of Social Security. The table below summarizes the impact of Kemp-Roth upon variously situated taxpayers in 1984 (on the assumption of a 9.2 percent rate of inflation between 1981 and 1984).

Income (Thousands of dollars)	Average Tax Cut	Average Tax Increase Due to Bracket Creep and Social Security	Average Net Change in Tax Liability	% Change in Tax Liability	% of all Taxpayers
Under $10	$84	$209	+ $125	+ 27.7%	33.3%
10–15	367	450	+ 83	+ 4.7	14.9
15–20	616	634	+ 18	+ 0.6	12.2
20–30	978	952	− 26	− 0.6	19.1
30–50	1,742	1,652	− 84	− 1.1	15.4
50–100	3,930	3,174	− 756	− 4.9	4.1
100–200	9,299	4,891	− 4,408	− 11.4	0.7
200–plus	25,604	6,177	− 19,427	− 15.1	0.2

Seldom do statistics speak less ambiguously. In plain language, Kemp-Roth will not, by any reasonable assumption, leave the 61 percent of the taxpaying public with incomes below $20,000 better off in 1984 than they were at the triumphant moment in August 1981 when Ronald Reagan affixed his signature to a legislative victory few had predicted. As for the more prosperous one out of five with incomes between $30,000 and $50,000, their average reward will amount to a whopping $84. On the other hand, if you are an income aristocrat, Kemp-Roth and its adornments convey golden implications. The 0.7 percent, seven of every thousand Americans, who reside in the $100,000–$200,000 bracket will typically add $4,408 or 11 percent of current after-tax income to their net proceeds. The $200,000-plus folks, two of every thousand, fare best of all.

They stand to gain an average $19,427, a pleasing 15.1 percent bonus.

Kemp-Roth amounts to genuine tax reduction for 5 percent of Americans at the top of the national income distribution and a tax increase for most of the remainder of the population. Approximately 85 percent of the benefits will accrue to taxpayers above annual incomes of $50,000. This is supply-side economics with a vengeance, a wager on the behavior of the already affluent. If the rich do their job, a new investment boom and a new surge of entrepreneurial innovation will vastly accelerate growth and allow its benefits to trickle down from the intrepid, gifted minority to humbler Americans, less individually and financially gifted.

Those who enjoy large incomes face problems special to their financial status, selection of the best devices for conversion of income into wealth and transmission of that wealth to chosen heirs undiminished by the IRS. An excellent protection of current income is any definition that turns it into capital gains. At the simplest level, a capital gain is the difference between two prices, a security bought at $50 and sold at $70, a home purchased for $80,000 and sold at twice that sum, an "old master" acquired at a mere $200,000 and auctioned for $900,000, and so on. Even before 1981's tax changes, capital gains were subject to a maximum tax of a mere 28 percent, little more than half the 50 percent maximum impost upon wages and salaries. That rate will now decline further toward 20 percent, a figure which is smaller than the marginal income and Social Security tax rates paid on its earnings from work by a family at the $15,000 mark. Even from the perspective of supply-siders, this reduction is open to dispute. It will in all probability do little to encourage productive efforts. Almost certainly it will add vastly to the publicly worthless attractions of real estate tax shelters and impart renewed impetus to speculation in collectibles.

One form of immortality, it is said, is that of the germ plasm. Another, perhaps, is associated with the transfer of property.

Estate taxation has been historically light in this country. Congress in 1981 acted almost to eliminate it, by exempting entirely bequests to spouses, whatever their size. In general, 1981 will be recalled as the year when the White House and a complaisant Congress engaged in large-scale income redistribution, from the bottom 60 percent to the top 5 percent of the population. No single action will more surely promote concentration of wealth than its amendment, almost as an afterthought, of inheritance taxation.

II

In recent years the complementary spectacle of stagnant or actually declining American manufacturing productivity and spectacular Japanese advances in American and other markets has inspired numerous explanations including a great deal of faddish attention to the group solidarity alleged to characterize corporate life in Japan, guarantees of lifetime employment, and loyalty of executives to their initial corporate employers. Although they may differ on most other points of comparison between the two economies, the diagnosticians take common alarm over the failures of major American producers to replace aging equipment and keep abreast of the technological state of the art. As a percentage of Gross National Product, America spends far less on machines and structures (capital formation) than Japan, Germany, and most of the rest of Western Europe. The phenomenon is all the more disquieting because in important instances, such as statistical quality control, robot technology, and continuous casting in steel, innovation was American in origin, neglected at home, and honored abroad.

The sociology of innovation and investment is mysterious. During most of the last century British engineers and industrialists dominated international markets for capital and consumer goods. In the 1880s for no adequate reason these aggressive, thrusting souls lost their élan, became complacent, and gradually lost ground to American and German rivals. Conceivably, the United States is replaying that old British song.

Supply-siders explain American malaise quite differently. Practically everybody is to blame except businessmen. Ordinary Americans save too little and spend too much. Affluent citizens who do most of the saving that actually occurs will save much more if outrageously high marginal taxes on their incomes are reduced. Because saving is sparse, interest rates are high and the cost of capital discouraging to potential investment. The heaviest savers, favorites of both the Deity and Jerry Falwell, can be found in the $50,000-and-above brackets who collectively save 35 percent of after-tax income.[6] The president and Congress acted wisely to shower this valuable group with most of the benefits of tax reduction.

Demagogues in Washington and a misled public have imposed other handicaps upon American corporations. Their astute leaders carefully compare the cost of borrowed money (much too high because of Democratic discouragement of savers), with the profits to be expected from the capital equipment it is used to acquire (far too low because of other government policies). Regulation, the theme of chapter 4, has diverted resources from productive uses to profitless acquisition of equipment and redesign of facilities in obedience to the mandates of incompetent bureaucrats.

Just as high marginal rates discourage saving, IRS treatment of depreciation exerts malignant pressure against investment and in favor of the mergers and acquisitions that entertained the public in the summer of 1981 and later. Most enterprises depend upon the accumulation of depreciation allowances, the sums

---

[6] See the *Wall Street Journal,* July 15, 1981, p. 26. Families who stagger along with incomes under $10,000 engage in negative saving: they supplement meager earnings with borrowing and public benefits.

they can legally subtract from income subject to taxation, to finance replacements for creaky equipment and obsolete factories and mills.

The more quickly the tax administrators permit recovery of investment costs, the smaller is the risk attached to the acquisition and the lower is the price of a superior replacement, on the reasonable assumption that inflation will continue into the predictable future. Furthermore, the simpler depreciation accounting for tax purposes can be made, the less time and money will be wasted on lawyers, accountants, and computer specialists. According to such criteria, pre-Reagan tax policy flunked. Depreciation was enormously complicated because IRS classified capital assets according to the duration of their expected useful lives, as defined by engineering estimates. These frequently unrealistically disregarded the likelihood, especially in technologically vigorous industries, that long before machines wore out they became obsolescent. Newer and better equipment shortens the economic lives of machines in excellent engineering health, incompletely depreciated yet financially worthless.

Even if such calamities are averted, the minimum effect of the useful life criterion is proliferation of vast numbers of subcategories of equipment and structures and definition of chronologies that stretch from two and a half to sixty years. Always a burden, this cumbersome procedure inflicts acute pain during spells of actual and anticipated inflation. Allowed to write off a $10 million milling device over a 10-year period, a machine maker will find that its replacement may be priced two or three times higher. Corporations, as a result, pay taxes on fictitious profits, some of which should be treated as an addition to deductible depreciation in compensation for inflation.

It is an affecting brief for corporate America. For those whose hearts are moved by the pitiable plight of private enterprise, it must be almost miraculous that any investment at all takes place in the face of such political discouragement and harassment. Even before Reagan, conservative Democrats and Republicans were proposing remedies.[7]

Like Kemp-Roth, administration business tax alterations seem to be fair and attractive, not least because they simplify complex regulations. "Ten-five-three," the nickname for new depreciation policy, groups most capital items into three categories. With some exceptions, buildings will henceforth be written off in 10 years instead of current 25 to 60-year time spans, equipment in 5 years instead of 5 to 35, and cars and light trucks in 3 years. What a break for aggressive businessmen! Although the Treasury stands to lose an estimated $40 billion each year, investment should be vastly stimulated to the joy of America and the dismay of Japan.

Could any artifact of the political process possibly be more clearly in the national interest? Well, yes. For starters, about 80 percent of the tax savings will flow to the 1,700 largest American corporations that during the last twenty years have generated only 4 percent of all new employment opportunities,[8] possibly because their presiding geniuses have been preoccupied with financial manipulation instead of research and development. There is no guarantee that with additional funds to play with, the inhabitants of executive suites will not multiply takeover efforts, divert cash flow to foreign ventures, or simply enlarge dividend payments to the stockholders.

---

[7]Before dissolving into tears, skeptics will recall that the investment tax credit, a Kennedy legacy, extends 10 percent discounts on new capital equipment and that in its wisdom Congress has offered an array of benefits to builders, miners, and explorers for oil and gas. Most industries as a result paid far less than the 46 percent corporate profit rate on their earnings. Even before 1981 tax changes, such high technology industries as semiconductors were permitted to write off new investment in periods as short as three years. In many if not most instances, taxes on corporate profits actually are paid by customers in the form of higher prices.

[8]I have drawn upon the valuable analysis of Citizens for Tax Justice, in particular their March 19, 1981 release.

There is justification for writing off high technology investment much more quickly than the five years in the new legislation and the IRS, as earlier noted, has routinely negotiated such
arrangements. However, in many other industries shortened
depreciation will load the dice against needed long-range commitments in plant and equipment and for alternatives with
short life expectancies. The combination of rapid write-off and
continuing tax credits will in some instances generate tax subsidies—the sum of credits and allowable depreciation will exceed
net income.

One of the fastest growing and least useful of American
industries is the design of tax shelters, in which fast depreciation constitutes a major structural element. These will further
proliferate in activities like equipment leasing, hotels, shopping
centers, restaurants, and amusement parks, none of them essential to the revitalization of the economy, all of them rivals for
scarce savings. According to one expert, the shelter business
merits "its own line in the GNP accounts."[9] Nowhere is this
more likely than in real estate. Here the name of the game has
long been conversion of comparatively heavily taxed ordinary
income into lightly assessed capital gains. Faster depreciation
will enlarge short-run capital gains for sellers and then enable
buyers to start the depreciation clock ticking again, so that they
can reap similar gains. The shelter game inflates construction
prices, distorts capital allocations, and rewards speculators
rather than investors.

In sum, 10-5-3 is a strategy ill conceived to stimulate
substantial quantities of additional investment and still less
likely to encourage investment in productive uses. Nor is it neutral in its handling of enterprises of differing size, or hostile to
speculative uses of available savings. It is a handout in the
same spirit as Kemp-Roth: the big fare much better than the
small.

---

[9]The words are those of Harvard's Dale Jorgenson from whom we shall hear more
shortly.

III

The supply-side argument, as we have seen, makes its case for tax breaks tilted toward the least needy on incentive grounds. It is a case that cries for close inspection. Who actually needs incentives to work harder, spend less, and save more? Who has gained from inflation and who has lost? Whose taxes accordingly should be slashed most compassionately? The comparisons in the accompanying table convey answers to these relevant queries quite different from those of the Reagan administration.[10]

Running as hard as it could, the typical American family barely held its own *pretax* and, because of rising Social Security levies and bracket creep, endured severe erosion of *after-tax* income. Their financial betters not only kept abreast of inflation but gratifyingly improved their incomes.

WHO NEEDS A TAX BREAK?

	% Increase 1972–1980	% Increase in Excess of Inflation
Inflation	79	—
Median family income	79	0
Average hourly earnings	80	1
Personal dividend income	126	47
After-tax corporate profits	174	95
Corporate executive pay	176	97
Personal interest income	217	138

Owners and managers have profited from inflation. Lesser breeds on assembly lines and in offices have suffered losses. The contrast raises a sensitive issue for supply-side enthusiasts. If executives in particular have prospered so mightily in the land, why hasn't the American economy performed better and diffused its benefits more widely? Any adherent to the true free

---

[10]I have drawn upon the *Economic Report of the President*, January 1981, pp. 236, 253, 255, 274.

market credo admits that large rewards for any economic actor derive their legitimacy only from high productive contributions to GNP. One does not want to be gratuitously unpleasant, but it is difficult to view with equanimity the trend of some events in autos, steel, textiles, shoes, consumer electronics, and railroads, among other faltering industries whose leaders have rewarded themselves far more lavishly than their employees. One of the less emphasized differences between American and Japanese systems of remuneration is the much narrower spread between top and bottom in the latter than in the former. Can it be that we pay our managers too much?

As with executive salaries, so also with corporate profits and dividends. These also justify themselves only in association with gains in productivity, quality and variety, and growth of GNP. During the 1970s these were scant or absent, and, accordingly, the rewards of managers and owners should have declined, not risen.

Evidently there is no reason to further enlarge benefits for groups who, blessed with ample earlier emoluments, have conspicuously neglected to deliver the goods for which they were lavishly compensated. Why not instead, on grounds both of incentive and equity, concentrate tax reductions on the losers in the race against inflation: Americans of working-class status?

Like other human endeavors, some types of bribery are more efficient than others. Students of the subject know that before the unmarked bills are transferred, reasonable assurance should be available that they will encourage desired actions. Depreciation reform in the Reagan manner amounts to an annual $40 billion bribe to the business community without the least guarantee of improved performance.

As a whole, the White House and Congress have collaborated in the creation of a tax program that scandalously violates accepted canons of fairness without credibly promoting saving, investment, and work effort.

Genuine tax reform awaits a more enlightened president and Congress than the current offenders. It is not difficult to sketch some of the items on an agenda aimed at improvement of both equity and efficiency. As far as tax treatment of depreciation goes, the simplest change would allow enterprises to write off the entire cost of new equipment and structures in the year in which it is incurred. Naturally, specialists have proposed much fancier alternatives. At Harvard, Dale Jorgenson and Alan Auerbach have designed a beautifully intricate way of compensating for the impact of inflation on investment cost recovery.[11] In the presence of political will, equitable reform is technically simple.

A word next about tax shelters. All parties, except possibly their beneficiaries, deplore tax shelters as a waste of expensive energy and distortion of resource allocation. Friends of the rich, never more numerous than now, argue that the way to discourage the hunt of the affluent for tax shelter is to cut their taxes so deeply that the rewards of tax avoidance will be worth less than the efforts devoted to creating shelters.

Why not instead eliminate the tax shelters on grounds of public health? Most of them could be dismantled by a single, momentous simplification of the tax code: assessment for tax purposes of capital gains in precisely the same fashion as income from any other source. What a gain in efficiency! Evidence is abundant in testimonials to the economically damaging effects of long-standing indulgence to capital gains. For the most part, the tax benefits reward successful speculation in real estate, commodities, and common stocks. Only exceptionally are they appropriate tokens of public gratitude for the risks entailed in innovation. Legions of tax lawyers and public accountants would be manumitted for far more sensible activities

---

[11]Jorgenson and Auerbach also allow corporate investors to deduct allowable depreciation in the first year of life of the new investment, but they estimate "allowable depreciation" by continued reference to the usable life of the machine. Vociferous in its cheers for the Reagan revolution, *Fortune* praised the Jorgenson-Auerbach alternatives and scolded the corporate community: "Business's dismal record of putting its parochial interest above the general good is the darkest cloud over Washington's new approach to taxes." (March 9, 1971, p. 96.) Couldn't have said it better myself.

than redefining ordinary income as capital gains.[12]

Our experiment between 1972 and 1980 in bribing the affluent has failed. Perhaps we have been offering financial help to the wrong people. When an American Mitterand gets his chance to shape national policy, he might well start as the living Mitterand actually has started in France, with benefits for humbler folk. Consider those at the bottom of the American income distribution, families on welfare. The percentage of employable adults among them has always been far smaller than popular imagination fervently insists. Still there are some. The best possible stimulus to their work effort, the only route out of welfare dependency, is a negative income tax whose benefit reduction rate is low. Sensible welfare reform of this nature aids the working poor as well as AFDC clients. Accordingly, it eliminates temptations, unfortunately enhanced by congressional action in 1981, to improve a family's financial situation by leaving ill-paid jobs and collecting instead welfare and the supplements of Medicaid, food stamps, and housing subsidies.

Something can and should be done to make life more attractive for ordinary wage slaves, that large, amorphous majority grouped around the national median family income figure of $20,000. For many if not most of this group, their heaviest tax burden is the Social Security deduction from their paychecks.[13] Lower payroll taxes will generate important gains for wage earners, their employers, and the economy in general. For employees, any tax cut is the equivalent of a pay hike. For employers, reduced labor costs will, at least in competitive industries, translate into smaller price increases. And, although most Americans of moderate income save very little, there are so

---

[12]In the silly summer of 1981, major New York City law firms were hiring associates fresh out of law school at stipends of $42,000. These overachievers presumably merit such reward mostly as manipulators of the tax code on behalf of huge corporations and affluent individuals.

[13]The matching contribution by employers in most instances is a disguised, second deduction from take-home pay. Employers could afford to pay their employees more if this employment cost were reduced.

many of them that even trivial additions to the savings of millions of families mount up into the billions of dollars of new funds for investment.

In collaboration with the media, the Reagan Administration has terrified the public with nightmares of bankrupt Social Security trust funds in the imminent future. Pollsters regularly report apprehension among the young and middle-aged that by the time they become senior citizens, no green Treasury check will solace the golden years of retirement. The campaign's object has been preparation of the public and congressional mind for a series of curtailments certainly in future benefits and probably in those currently paid as well.[14]

As might be predicted, experts in and out of government quarrel about the date money for the old folks will run out. The argument is pointless. It is inconceivable that any Congress, even one dominated by Republicans and "boll weevils," would stop payment on the green checks that flow to Social Security pensioners. If the sums available from the Social Security trust funds become inadequate, they will be supplemented. That supplement need not and should not come from heavier deductions out of take-home pay.

The simple method of maintaining benefits *and* reducing payroll taxes echoes European practice by financing entitlements partly out of general tax revenue. The gain in equity is substantial, for the comparatively progressive personal income tax will partially substitute for heavily regressive imposts on wages and salaries.

As even Reagan supporters fear, broad tax cuts over three years may stimulate inflation more quickly and more substantially than saving and investment. There are more sensible ways to deploy taxes against inflation. One source of that inflation has been enormous escalation of housing prices. The tax code

---

[14]In 1981, the White House scored an early success by persuading Congress to eliminate the minimum $122 benefit. To its credit, Congress soon reconsidered and reinstated the benefit.

presently feeds speculation in new and old single-family houses by allowing deduction of interest on mortgage debt from taxable income. For someone in the 50 percent bracket, the cost of servicing his debt is cut in half and his incentive to acquire more expensive property correspondingly increased. To protect home owners of moderate means, it would be fair and sensible to cap the interest deduction at $200 per month.

One can dream. Complete elimination of allowable deductions for meals, tickets to theaters and sporting events, and trips to conventions in salubrious tourist resorts would diminish time now wasted by businessmen, improve both their character and productivity, and, for the public, lower the tab for a night on the town.

I sketch these implausible reforms out of not the least expectation that they will any time soon become a political reality. I make only the wistful point that justice and incentives to work and invest are more compatible than the theology of supply-side economics asserts.

3

fill it to the
rim with grim

The benefits to the average American will be striking. Inflation . . . will
be cut in half by 1986. The American economy will produce 13 million
new jobs by 1986, nearly three million more than if the status quo in
government policy were to prevail. The economy itself should break
out of its anemic growth patterns to a much more robust growth trend
of 4 to 5 percent a year. These positive results will be accomplished
simultaneously with reducing the tax burden, increasing private saving,
and raising the living standard of the American family.

AMERICA'S NEW BEGINNING:
A PROGRAM FOR ECONOMIC RECOVERY,
February 18, 1981

In 1980 Ronald Reagan ran strongly among union members
because he promised the good things epitomized in the quota-
tion from Stockman's black book. No evidence exists that the
40 percent or more of the blue-collar work force who deserted
Jimmy Carter clamored for smaller Social Security pensions,
tighter eligibility criteria for unemployment benefits, elimination of trade adjustment payments to men and women laid off
because of rising imports, and more dangerous factory environments.

The unemphasized or unmentioned elements of the Reagan

message were news that the price of less inflation, more jobs, and rising living standards—pie in the sky by and by—was immediate redirection of public spending priorities, revision of the tax code, drastic rearrangement of federal-state relations, reduced regulation of business, and monetary tactics calculated to raise interest rates to punitive heights.

The spending, taxing, and deregulatory initiatives of Reagan's domestic agenda base themselves on the argument that the tax code discourages saving, investment, and work effort, that the environmental and other regulators dramatically enlarge business costs and divert investment away from productive outlets, and that welfare and other assistance to the losers in the American celebration is so lavish as to discourage beneficiaries to seek work and become independent.

None of these assertions can withstand factual inspection. Taxes on business profits and capital gains have been steadily declining. Generous investment incentives have been offered as far back as the Kennedy investment tax credit. Congress has assiduously protected high earners by enacting numerous deductions, exemptions, and tax shelters. The bulk of social expenditures flows to veterans and the elderly, not to families on welfare and food stamps. The costs of regulatory policy are drastically exaggerated and its benefits frequently ignored. More will be said subsequently on all of these points. Suffice it here to conclude that the unsatisfactory recent record of the American economy cannot be intelligibly explained in supply-side terms.

In the modern world, economic and political counterrevolutions spell themselves in the minutiae of government documents and statistical reports. In its endless detail, the federal budget demands comprehensive skills of exegesis akin to those of Talmudic scholars. However, life is short and full of activities more stimulating than contemplation of endless rows and columns of numbers. Fortunately, succor is available from those who compile the numbers, the Office of Management and Budget. Jimmy Carter's final budget, a document now of mostly archeological interest, divided federal expenditures into five major categories. Of the federal dollar, national defense took 25 cents, direct benefit payments to individuals 48 cents, net interest on the federal debt 10 cents, grants to states and localities 8 cents, and other federal activities 9 cents.

For some years Social Security has constituted the largest single federal outlay and the bulk of direct benefit payments to individuals. Americans own most of the trillion dollar national debt. Hence interest on that sum consists largely of transfers from Americans who own no government bonds to those who do. Grants to states and localities, many of them progeny of the Great Society, are targeted at specific groups—children, handicapped, persistently unemployed, Spanish-speaking, and otherwise vulnerable individuals.

Each of these "categorical" federal initiatives has a history. The health of migrants, for example, is almost self-evidently a problem of national concern. Immigrants, legal or otherwise, are heavily concentrated in some cities and regions; so also are unskilled and sketchily educated American citizens who live in northern cities. Regional equity justifies financial sharing, possible only through national action, of the costs of providing public services for people who consume them more heavily than average residents.

Many federal programs responded to patterns of state and local discrimination against women, blacks, Hispanics, the elderly, and the disabled. On occasion, localities neglected completely those in greatest need, such as the completely disabled or the victims of child abuse. Still other categorical programs reflected shifting national priorities. During the 1950s, for example, in the post-Sputnik era, public support was strong enough for improved science education to elicit such a program from the conservative Eisenhower Administration.

Almost invariably the federal government enjoys the best sources of revenue. Unlike states and cities, it needn't balance its annual budget. Washington is in a position to redistribute tax revenue from booming parts of the country to those in distress. Localities with the most acute problems of shrinking employment and activity can least afford to cope with them because their tax base shrinks in step with the decline of manufacturing and service income.

Categorical programs have proliferated in the last two decades not because power-mad bureaucrats have subverted the tradition of local control and individual responsibility, but because the federal government has deployed more resources to cope with the difficulties of constituencies neglected or unfairly treated by local governments. For that powerful reason, money from Washington has invariably been accompanied by some degree of federal supervision.

Of the categorical grant issue, more later. To return to the budget's broad classifications, one can simplify even the Carter divisions of the federal dollar. Two functions dominate federal expenditure: national defense and income maintenance, the lion's share of the latter, Social Security pensions. Serious debate necessarily focuses on the relative size of the two.

A preliminary word is in order about the other side of the budget. The tax code presents itself in a set of volumes even more profitable to lawyers and accountants than the spending counterpart is to lobbyists and specialists in the composition of grant proposals. It too yields readily to simplification. Of the Treasury's revenue dollar, 45 cents comes from taxes on personal income, 29 cents from employee and employer contributions to Social Security trust funds, 9 cents from levies on corporate profits, another 9 cents from excises imposed on cigarettes, gasoline, liquor, and other consumer items, 4 cents from borrowing, and the missing 4 cents from "other," a label that covers receipts from sales of oil leases on federal properties, charges for use of public lands, and tariff collections.

Of the major revenue sources, only the personal income tax, though riddled by loopholes, can be considered mildly progressive. It extracts both more dollars *and* a larger percentage of the incomes taxed from those who earn rising sums of money.

Other taxes are regressive: they subtract fewer dollars but a larger percentage of income subject to tax as a worker's wage declines. An executive blessed with a salary of $200,000 contributes to Social Security only on the initial $30,000. If, as is likely, he (almost certainly) supplements this exiguous sum with interest, dividends, and capital gains, he will pay no Social Security at all on these or other types of property income.

Excises operate in much the same fashion. As incomes rise, so also do the fractions of them saved. Our $200,000 family will no doubt spend more than a less lucky $20,000 family on items subject to federal excise tax, but not ten times as much. The less affluent family will accordingly surrender a larger fraction of its smaller income than its luckier neighbor.

Close students of American taxation have concluded that over a broad range of incomes, the system—federal, state, and local—is approximately proportional. The progression in the federal and some state income levies just about cancels the regression embedded in federal payroll and excise taxes and the bulk of state and local tax arrangements. This is to say that if you are either quite poor or disgustingly rich, you stand in danger of paying slightly, but only slightly, steeper percentages of your income to tax collectors than the vast majority of your fellow Americans.

Just as tax labels tend to disguise instead of advertise their fairness or unfairness, spending classifications blandly conceal purpose and ideological justification. Try relabeling Social Security "welfare for the elderly" and defense spending "preparation for World War III" and note the contrasting emotional overtones. It is, one ought to concede, a virtue of Reagan reclassifications that, far more candidly than most earlier publications of the Office of Management and Budget, they declare intentions and valuations. In fact, they glare out of this simple table. Just in case the billions of dollars glazed vision, Mr. Stockman tells his story again, this time in percentages. Inevitably, all the numbers and percentages are guesses of varying plausibility about inflation and interest rates, military hardware prices, and the expense of the safety net.

SHIFT IN BUDGET PRIORITIES

	1981	1984
Dollar Amount (billions)		
DOD—military	$157.9	$249.9
Safety net programs	239.3	313.0
Net interest	64.3	66.8
All other	193.2	142.0
	$654.7	$771.6
Outlay Shares (percent)	*1981*	*1984*
DOD—military	24.1%	32.4%
Safety net programs	36.6	40.6
Net interest	9.8	8.6
All other	29.5	18.4
	100.0	100.0

Ah, the safety net, one of many administration gifts to the verbal currency of political argument. It defines the social protection asserted to be compatible with the efficient operation of a free enterprise economy populated with self-respecting men and women able and eager to support themselves most of the time. Its major elements include Social Security and Medicare for the elderly, unemployment compensation (but with significant alterations in duration and eligibility standards), "cash benefits for the chronically poor," and "society's obligations to veterans." An unexpected added starter is Head Start, the lone survivor from the Great Society. Social Security and unemployment benefits date back to the Social Security Act of 1935. We have been coddling veterans since the end of the eighteenth century. Most of the monies designated to keep the safety net in good repair will flow to middle-class and working-class beneficiaries. Of the remainder, far more will be paid to upper income recipients than to the poor.

The distribution of safety net outlays contrasts sharply with the programs comprised in "all other," the designated target of the Stockman axe. Here skulk the bureaucratic children of the War on Poverty—food stamps, legal services for the poor, Medicaid, school lunches, special nutrition programs for women, infants, and young children, Meals on Wheels for the housebound, subsidized housing, Title 1 subventions to public schools in low-income neighborhoods, public jobs and job training, and special education programs for handicapped youngsters.

Revisions in school lunch funding exemplify OMB attitudes. Until September 1981, the standard objective was provision of one-third of a child's nutritional needs at lunch. For a great many of these youngsters, lunch is the best, sometimes the only, meal of the day. The Department of Agriculture's own studies conclude that needy children derive between a third and a half of basic nutrition from this meal. They will have to feed themselves elsewhere. In the new order, pickle relish and catsup count as vegetables, jam masquerades as a serving of fruit, cookies and cake define themselves as bread, and the egg in the cake substitutes for meat. A hearty lunch for an adolescent might be two slices of cheese, one-fourth of a cup of grape juice, one cupcake, a cup of whole milk (four not eight ounces) and a quarter-cup of canned peaches.[1]

Children are particularly vulnerable also to the tightening of eligibility standards for welfare, curtailments of food stamp allotments, and elimination of special feeding programs for infants, young children, and their mothers. Right-to-lifers, prominent among the budget cutters, cherish fetuses. They might spare a thought and an appropriation for the children that fetuses often become.

Not even their sturdiest admirers will privately deny that some of these efforts overlap. Others were poorly designed or

---

[1] See the *New York Times,* September 14, 1981, p. A 19. In response to general outrage, the administration at least temporarily withdrew the changes in nutritional standards.

poorly administered. Almost all of them have been underfunded through their comparatively brief histories. Nevertheless, the categorical programs of the Great Society succeeded,
if only to a limited degree, in extending middle class benefits
and entitlements downward in the income pyramid to the genuinely poor. Since, among the poor, blacks are disproportion-
ately numerous, the Great Society's spending programs may
have done even more to promote black interests than its civil
rights legislation.

As good Social Darwinists know, the improvement of the
breed is tough on the weak and sickly. In accord with nature's
intentions, the poor should and will suffer for their financial
failures. God and Reagan will continue to maintain the middle
class in their current station and coddle the genuinely wealthy
even more lovingly than the Democrats. New funds will deluge
the Pentagon in megabillions almost numerous enough to purchase all the lethal toys upon which our chiefs of staff have set
their loyal hearts. The percentages tell a stark tale. In 1984 (the
timing seems especially appropriate), military spending will
absorb nearly a third of the federal budget instead of its present
quarter. Between 1981 and 1986, the Pentagon will have a cool
trillion dollars to play with. By contrast, "all other" will shrink
from 29.5 percent to 18.4 percent.

If one is to believe Stockman's happy calculators, five years
from now the federal share of the Gross National Product will
contract to 19 percent, down from 1981's 23 percent. In 1984, a
year hard to avoid, the federal budget will balance and two
years onward a surplus of $30 billion will be registered. In the
dismal autumn of 1981, Mr. Reagan openly admitted that, alas
for the nation, the budget would not be balanced after all by
1984.

Later in our chronicle, considerably more will be said about
the implausibility of these forecasts. Suffice it here to indicate
a single major ground for skepticism: the inflationary impact of
defense spending. As the MIT economist Lester Thurow has
pointed out, "the military build-up that is currently being con-

templated is three times as large as the one that took place during the Vietnam War."[2] That buildup, it ought not be forgotten, gave birth to expectations of inflation and a price-wage spiral that plague the economy to the present moment.

In contrast, of course, with Lyndon Johnson's desperate attempt to enlarge military and social expenditures simultaneously, this administration intends to dismantle much of the welfare state, a budgetary necessity that coincides delightfully with ideological preference.

Administration ideologues do not rest their case merely on asserted needs to rebuild the strength of the armed services. "All other" deserves severe pruning on its own demerits. The misguided Washington social planners, expelled like so many money changers from the temples of government, inflicted serious damage upon the incentive—each person for him or herself —to strive for individual salvation. Misguided generosity, mistaken entitlements to federal charity, served only to prolong the dependency of a welfare population which needed, even deserved, better treatment.

The supply-siders, at less lofty levels of social doctrine, level other criticisms at Democratic blunders. All too often, so they claim, benefits flow to the unneedy. Until 1977 some college students collected food stamps and stamps still are available to families with incomes substantially higher than the poverty line, the implicit administration definition of true need. Because school lunches partially duplicate food stamps, some lucky youngsters gorge themselves on four instead of three meals at taxpayer expense. As the indictment continues, programs for poor people in general and Medicaid especially have been blemished by administrative mismanagement and frequent fraud.

A rich menu of overlapping entitlements has occasionally shoved the recipients of multiple subsidies well above the income level of hardworking, fully employed men and women.

---

[2]See the *New York Review of Books,* May 14, 1981, p. 3.

Finally, bureaucratic Washington administration of narrowly defined categorical grants erodes state and local home rule, generates webs of red tape, and arbitrarily ignores significant variations in local needs and individual circumstances.

The response from beleaguered partisans of the Great Society is as familiar as the complaints of the supply-siders. It is a challenge to improve the means rather than jettison the objectives. If programs overlap, redesign and simplification are appropriate. Better administrators can be hired to improve efficiency, wring out waste, and bring to justice the perpetrators of fraud, many of them more or less respected members of the medical profession. As for local control, two responses are readily available. Most categorical grants were in fact negotiated by mayors and governors with the detested Washington bureaucrats. And, never to be forgotten, federal responsibility expanded as states and local governments failed to serve increasing numbers of their most vulnerable residents.

Not approving in the first place of most attempts to aid the usual Great Society client, the Reagan approach to the programs excluded from the safety net is radically different. Believing that many are at best unnecessary and at worst injurious to their intended beneficiaries, the Office of Management and Budget has sought to eliminate some and severely prune the remainder. The $36 billion of budget reductions, a 1981 administration triumph, are sums squeezed almost completely from appropriations targeted at low-income Americans.

The targets were shrewdly chosen. Among conservatives, food stamps are nearly as unpopular as welfare. Without commenting nastily on the shallowness of the wells of compassion among supply-siders, it is genuinely difficult to explain why improving the diets of hungry adults and alleviating malnutrition among their children should arouse such gusts of rage. Part of the explanation may derive from the public use of food stamps by their recipients. Working class and middle income shoppers at checkout counters cannot help noticing people using food stamps to purchase items as expensive as the contents of their own carts. The reaction is mean-spirited. Cash can be squandered on hard liquor and easy women. Food stamps nourish poor children.

For partisans of the work ethic unblinded by prejudice, food stamps exhibit an additional merit. Their amount declines as the income of those who collect them rises. Food stamps are a social program that has worked: hunger is a much rarer phenomenon in America than it was a decade and a half ago. Even though the 1981 cost to the Treasury approximated $12 billion, the maximum benefit is a modest $2 per person per day and average benefits have been running at $1.32 per person per day —44 cents a meal.

Food stamps are a model of administrative efficiency because their objective is clear and attainable: alleviating hunger and malnutrition. Unquestionably some middle class families have manipulated the system to their personal benefit. Of what public or private activity is such a statement untrue? Nevertheless, in 1981 an average food stamp family earned only $3,900. Sixty percent had no savings, two-thirds did not own a car, and 71 percent lived in rented quarters.

None of these well-known facts deterred the budget cutters, determined to save a couple of billion dollars. They proceeded to do so by tactics that recalled the Carter Administration's justly celebrated propensity for shooting itself in the foot. There is some justification in conservative logic for subtracting school lunches from food stamp allocations. Why, after all, should a mother whose three children are in school enjoy more favorable benefits than a sister with three preschool youngsters? Of course a more generous correction of such anomalies would be an increase in benefits for the second family.

But how by administration logic is its reduction of allocations to the working poor to be justified? It starts from the premise that families who don't really need them now collect food stamps. At first presentation, the charge appears reasonable. Under Carter rules, families became ineligible for food stamps only when their income[3] reached $14,000, more than 50 percent above the current poverty line. Reagan's OMB lowered the ceiling to $11,000, still 30 percent above the poverty line.

Thrifty certainly, sensible no. An example will illuminate the impact. Consider the situation of a woman with three children and no adult male on the scene. If she has a job at $5.25 an hour, she qualified (pre-Reagan) for $99 in food stamps. If a generous employer rewards her with an extra dime an hour, she will, under Reagan revisions, lose her food stamp eligibility. Ten cents an hour is $208 a year. Her food stamp loss totals $1,188. The marginal tax rate on her $208 is about 500 percent. This, remember, is an administration deeply troubled by the assertedly adverse impact upon incentives to work of marginal tax rates of the order of 40 or 50 percent.

In the jargon of social administration, Stockman and company have enmeshed themselves, possibly without noticing, in the "notch dilemma." A "notch" surfaces whenever an extra dollar of income triggers loss of *more* than a benefit dollar. Thus when reduced income ceilings are imposed on housing aid, Medicaid, and other income-tested benefits, a welfare mother or an adult male earning no more than the minimum wage, would need to act irrationally in order to accept promotion or seek work if not presently employed.

Intentionally or otherwise, OMB's redesign of the food stamp program assaults precisely the work incentives cherished by the administration from the president downward. The heaviest impact will be endured not by the welfare population, which will continue to be eligible for benefits, but for those who by their own efforts have managed to stay just perilously above the poverty level.

The budget crisis derives from the poor productivity record of the economy, particularly in the last decade. Students of productivity tend to be more certain that per capita output now

---

[3]Unless otherwise specified, the families discussed consist of four persons.

rises more slowly than it did for most of this country's history as an independent state, than they are about the causes of the phenomenon. Among the usual suspects are the increase in energy costs, the burdens of regulation, and the continuing shift of employment from manufacturing—where productivity gains are comparatively easy to achieve—to services, where it is much harder to achieve parallel results. At Columbia University, Seymour Melman, an economist and engineer, has made an impressive case against the defense sector as the consumer and waster of inordinate numbers of scientists, engineers, and skilled workmen. Some, among them myself, note that American managers in recent years have scanted research and development and devoted their talents to corporate mergers and financial manipulations.

Sluggish productivity, however explained, slows or halts the rise of average income from work, and makes tax burdens heavier than otherwise they would need to be to finance defense and social expenditures. The tax rebellion signalized by California Proposition 13 and Massachusetts's more recent Proposition 2 1/2 is fueled by the resentment of working and middle class families whose budgets have been under heavier and heavier pressure.

Neglect of the administration's stated principles is even more blatant in its approach to welfare. Three presidents—Richard Nixon, Gerald Ford,[4] and Jimmy Carter—tried fruitlessly to transform Aid to Families with Dependent Children (AFDC), welfare in short, into a completely federally funded entitlement, emphasizing national standards of eligibility, administration, work requirements, and benefits.

As matters stand, cumbersome combinations of state and local administration and funding have created enormous inequities and tremendous disparities among the states in the treatment of similarly situated families. About half the states deny benefits to families in which both parents are present. By

---

[4]President Ford never sent his Income Supplement Plan (ISP) to Congress.

so doing, they offer a strong incentive to fathers to desert their wives and children in order to improve their families' financial situation. The size of cash allotments differs widely according to the politics, prevailing wage levels, and intensity of racial feeling in assorted jurisdictions. The least generous states, almost entirely in the South, have exported in the last generation a large percentage of their welfare population to the North and Midwest where standards of support have been comparatively generous. The sheer accident of geography determines the fate of young children, a majority of the welfare clientele. Some will be raised in conditions of severe privation. Others will benefit from adequate nutrition, medical care, and housing.

As long as states can define their own standards of need and even determine the percentage of those that they decide to fund, politically reactionary legislatures and governors will be in a position to push their neediest citizens into the direction of communities less barbarously inclined. So long as Americans enjoy the constitutionally protected right to travel, welfare is a national problem, for no state can deny entry and needed public assistance to migrants from the remainder of the country. Federal assumption of state and local shares of welfare and Medicaid would enormously improve the fiscal condition of Frost Belt states and eliminate unwholesome political temptations to compete for new industry by reducing social programs to facilitate tax breaks for business.[5]

Few serious students of welfare dispute the desirability of federalization. Easier said than done. All attempts to eliminate existing anomalies endeavor to reconcile three objectives. Benefits ought, in the first place, to be adequate to support the needy in socially acceptable conditions. Next, strong work incentives should be offered to encourage employable adults to

---

[5] In 1975, when New York City teetered on the brink of bankruptcy, its deficit just about matched the amounts the city spent for welfare and Medicaid. Most states pay the complete nonfederal share of these benefits. New York splits that share between the state and localities.

seek and keep jobs. Finally, program costs must not exceed publicly acceptable totals.

Nixon's FAP (Family Assistance Program) and Carter's PBJI (Program for Better Jobs and Incomes) both endorsed the negative income tax as the crucial disbursement mechanism.[6] As the term implies, the responsible government agency, possibly the Internal Revenue Service, will mail checks to eligible families without income. As a family's income from work rises, the size of benefits diminishes but by an amount *less* than earnings. Invariably work improves total income, simply because the benefit reduction rate is below 100 percent.

At precisely this juncture, the trio of objectives begins to clash. Stipulate, for example, a basic cash benefit payment of $8,000 to a family of four, approximately the official poverty line. Any employable adult in the household should of course be encouraged to work. The fewer benefits he (or more likely she) must surrender by entering the labor market, the greater the stimulus to do so. If benefits declined only $1 for each $4 earned, $1,000 of income from casual work would add $750 to the initial $8,000.

The stimulus to work effort undoubtedly is substantial but there is an equally pronounced expansion of the proportion of the population rendered eligible for benefits and, consequently, of program costs. The arithmetic is grim, especially for partisans of public economy. Our hypothetical family would receive some public help until its earned income touched $32,000—60 percent higher than the national median in 1981, and coincidentally just about the average earnings of the air traffic controllers victimized by the Reagan administration in the summer of 1981.[7]

---

[6]Its ideological origin is impeccably conservative. Milton Friedman advocated a negative income tax as a substitute for cash payments and benefits in kind more than two decades ago.

[7]With no one working, the family gets its $8,000 cash benefit. A benefit reduction rate of 25 percent as here assumed would reduce the $8,000 by one dollar only when four dollars were earned. It follows that $32,000 must be earned before the $8,000 completely disappears.

Such an outcome is implausible financially and completely impossible politically. It is indeed a scheme, delightful to a very few equality freaks like myself, for substantial redistribution of income from the top 40 percent of the population to the bottom three-fifths. The social scientists who worked on FAP and PBJI necessarily compromised on the crucial issues of cash payment and benefit reduction rate.

They reached similar conclusions. The basic benefit rate was to be 50 percent of the poverty level and the same 50 was selected as the benefit reduction rate. Fiscally and politically the consequences are more acceptable, though still not palatable enough to be swallowed by Congress.[8] For one thing, cash benefits stopped at the poverty level. For another, a much smaller additional number of families became eligible.

But frustration even of this modest proposal exemplifies the difficulty of welfare reform. After all, 50 percent of the Washington definition of poverty, far from generous to begin with, did not impress all observers as a socially acceptable minimum. Critics asserted that the 50 percent benefit reduction rate was too high to stimulate job search. That figure, the highest rate applied to any portion of wages and salaries, is said to dampen incentives for more prosperous Americans.

Whatever their limitations, FAP and PBJI did emphasize encouragement to people on welfare and, in the Carter version, offered public jobs as a last resort. This administration substitutes sticks for carrots. Among the affluent, blaming the victim is a traditionally popular blood sport. Accordingly, no attempt is planned to alter the existing patchwork of funding and administrative inequities. The Reagan emphasis is upon tighter administration, stricter work requirements, and financial saving. A different assortment of anomalies arouses OMB concern from the disparities of benefit level and eligibility recognized by

---

[8]In 1970 and again in 1971 the House of Representatives passed FAP. On both occasions, the measure failed in the Senate. Carter's PBJI never emerged from committee as far as a vote on the floor of the House of Representatives.

Daniel Patrick Moynihan in the Nixon years and Joseph Califano at Health Education and Welfare in the Carter regime. Harken to OMB: "Anomalies in the present system often result in the payment of cash welfare grants to high-income families," among them "mothers and children without regard for the presence of a working stepparent in the home." The things that worry conservatives! Henceforth the income of a child's stepparent will be counted as a source of support. No end of worries for the budget warriors. They also seek to limit "deductible child care costs and standardize other work-related expenses." What's the problem? Well, "A family of four that receives $500 in monthly cash benefits because it had no other income could offset an additional $500 a month in earnings by charging off larger child care and other 'work-related expenses.' The family could then continue to receive its full monthly AFDC grant plus its $500 monthly earnings, for an annual total income of $12,000." How many families in fact mulct the taxpayers in this outrageous manner? OMB does not say.

Nevertheless, public suspicion of the honesty and industry of people on welfare is undoubtedly intense enough to attract political support for Reagan tactics, now as formerly. In his two California gubernatorial terms, Mr. Reagan experimented with "workfare." Adults were compelled to perform unpaid public work on pain of losing benefits. As a method of social discipline, coerced labor dates back to the reign of Queen Elizabeth I. From her day to Ronald Reagan's, such schemes have been expensive to administer, nuisances to supervisors, sources of little or no useful results, and occasions of resentment among public employees on regular payrolls. No evidence exists that "working off" benefits prepares these conscripts for normal participation in the job market. Nevertheless, if the president has his way, workfare will become one of the few nationally required elements of a welfare system otherwise chaotically diverse.

Food stamps and welfare exemplify the administration's social strategy. The OMB assault upon them deploys the weapons of lower income ceilings for eligibility, pruning of overlapping benefits, stricter identification of ineligible beneficiaries, and much administrative harassment. Regardless of need, money is to be saved. Thus, in anticipation of "comprehensive legislation" OMB opted for a ceiling upon the growth of Medicaid reimbursements to states and localities. State officials who may not completely appreciate their good fortune will receive, ready or not, "additional incentives to reduce fraud, waste, and abuse," not to mention powerful encouragement to reduce Medicaid costs by kicking as many low-income but fully employed families off the rolls as possible.

Some ingenious souls are at work in the budget office. They have faulted rent supplements as inequitable to those who do not receive them. As matters stand, the Department of Housing and Urban Development (HUD) extends "very deep subsidies to less than 9% of the total eligible households." Worse still, HUD allows tenants to pay no more than 25 percent of their adjusted incomes as rent at a time when "Many poor people do not live in subsidized housing; and more than 13 million renters at all levels of income have been paying a greater percentage of their incomes as rent in recent years." In short, if you cannot or will not provide for all, then refrain from helping anybody.

The administration does not limit application of its social vision to welfare families and other low-income Americans. Ordinary working stiffs also need a bracing dose of moral rehabilitation. For years, conservative economists have fretted about unemployment benefits as interferences with the operation of competitive labor markets. "Generous" unemployment compensation checks encourage men and women of flabby character to continue to collect them instead of moving to Texas or flipping Big Macs at a handy McDonald's. The issue is the more acute because, so OMB avers, aid to the unemployed has strayed far away from the intentions of presidents and Congresses, at least those around in the 1930s. Right now, whenever national unemployment among insured workers exceeds 4 percent, federal money becomes available to finance thirteen weeks of benefits in addition to the basic twenty-six weeks covered by state plans. Moreover, when the unemployment rate in any state exceeds 5 percent, this extension is automatically triggered, even though the national figure is below 4 percent.

Except in fits of absent-mindedness, Congress never meant to do more than shelter workers from deep income losses during brief spells of readjustment. The trouble now is that at the same time unemployment is "brief" in the Sun Belt it is protracted in Michigan and Ohio. As the grave government prose puts it, "Significant shifts in the U. S. economy over the last 15 years have produced significant regional differentials in unemployment regardless of general economic conditions. For example, in the depth of the 1974–75 recession, insured unemployment rates ranged from a high of 13.2% in Michigan to a low of 2.7% in Texas." As in 1975, so in 1981: "Today, while incurred unemployment is intolerably high in the industrial Northeast and Midwest, insured rates remain below 2% in a number of Sun Belt states."

Why worry? Well, the perverse "result is that the national trigger for extended benefits often provides . . . payments to workers in tight labor markets whenever the national trigger is on." An administration whose eye catches the fall of a sparrow if it is truly needy, frets about the existence of an occasional Texas slacker who, rather than accepting one of the numerous jobs readily available in a tight labor market, frivolously prefers to draw unemployment benefits for an additional thirteen weeks.

Easy to scoff. This administration means business. OMB intends "to recalibrate the extended benefits program in order to focus extended benefit payments only on those areas where high unemployment provides a real barrier to employment for unemployed workers." An even neater revision and stronger stimulus to job search is a proposed requirement that after thirteen weeks, people on unemployment benefits should accept jobs less skilled and worse paid than their work history might lead them to expect.[9]

There is more than one way to zap those who are not truly rich. As in the examples just cited, the direct strategy diminishes cash payments and other benefits. Much the same purpose is served by starving the places where low-income and working people cluster, cities under fiscal siege like Detroit, Boston, Philadelphia, Cleveland, Newark, Chicago, and the temporarily solvent Big Apple. Although communities in better financial shape will also be adversely affected, Reagan eliminations or reductions of funds for mass transit, community development, public housing, water treatment, neighborhood improvement, federally funded public jobs, and legal services for the poor, deliver a body blow to the urban economies of the Snow Belt.

Not only to them. A medium-sized city like Charlotte, North Carolina (1980 population 330,000) stood to lose in 1981 $45 million in federal grants and reimbursements, almost a quarter of its $185 million municipal budget. Its prospect of rescue by a legislature dominated by rural tobacco interests was minimal.[10]

Still another way to wound the weak is to reward the strong. Though distributed among the fifty states, the defense dollar migrates most substantially to major contractors like Boeing, Rockwell, Northrup, General Dynamics, and McDonnel-Douglas based in Texas, California, and other sunny environments. Much as tax reductions in 1981, 1982, and 1983 implicitly shift burdens from rich to poor people, simultaneous enlargement of weapons procurement and contraction of funds for urban projects adds new impetus to Sun Belt boom and Frost Belt decline.

---

[9] I have been quoting generously from that indispensable *vade mecum* OMB's *A Program for Economic Recovery*.
[10] My source is the *Economist* of London (May 30, 1981), a journal usually sympathetic to the Reagan approach to public administration.

If none of these techniques quite completes the wrecking of social services, the administration's final solution should finish the job. In the name of efficiency and home rule, OMB proposes to combine groups of specific, categorical grants into block programs, slash funding by 25 percent, and liberate governors and legislatures to set their own priorities within exceedingly broad boundaries. The education block, for example, incorporates Title I[11] grants for the disadvantaged, emergency school aid, basic skills improvement, adult education, preschool incentive grants for the handicapped, and education for the handicapped. Advocates of these constituencies are invited to fight each other in state capitols for bigger pieces of a shrunken pie.

The health blocks stimulate similar wholesome rivalries among those involved in control of high blood pressure, preventive care, fluoridation, rat control, family planning, treatment of venereal disease, and medical care of adolescents. For the most part, advocates of each program tend to treat colleagues as allies. Substitution of block grants will turn them, unless their self-restraint is heroic, into enemies.

As a final example, the plans for social services lump together eleven now separate endeavors: developmental disability care, rehabilitation services, Social Security, child welfare, foster care and adoptions, day care, social services training, child abuse, runaway and homeless youth, local initiatives, and "other." What hope for foster care or day care in legislatures controlled by suburban and rural interests? Or for limitation of child abuse? The politics of block grants are cynical and divisive, setting group against group, cities against states, and race against race.

After all, some wistful Reagan supporter might murmur, doesn't the safety net protect those in genuine need, "the truly needy," from destitution? In these hard times, none of us can

---

[11]This is shorthand for Title I of the Elementary and Secondary Education Act of 1965, a centerpiece of the Great Society's "unconditional" War against Poverty.

afford to be as compassionate as we would like to be. On inspection, unfortunately, the safety net turns out to be a textile construction of strange design, full of gaping holes and unneeded protections for the prosperous. As earlier noted, the Medicaid reimbursement ceiling combined with school lunch, food stamp, and rental supplement restrictions, will operate to damage the incomes both of welfare recipients and those employed at low wages. New York is reasonably representative of the national situation. A mother with two children who earns $592 each month, or nearly $4 an hour, collected (pre-Reagan) additional benefits worth $162, a total of $754. A nonworking mother received $542. The substantial difference, $212, operated as a work incentive.

Administration revisions leave the employed mother with only $555 after subtracting payroll taxes and such work-related expenses as travel, clothing, and lunches. A mother without paid work would fare as well or better. Her income would be $518, a trifling $37 less than her fully occupied sister. If welfare mothers are as rational as ordinary taxpayers, they will grasp the message without difficulty: stay home with the kids or arrange to get there just as soon as you can. It is worth displaying the disincentives of the administration's approach in their full horror.[12] Both faithful to the work ethic, Mrs. B will be forced down close to the poverty line and her still more enterprising sister Mrs. C below that line. The nonworker Mrs. A already subsisting in official poverty will lose less than her energetic sisters. As the authors of the study judiciously conclude, "Taken alone, each cut seems to be small enough to allow a recipient to absorb it with other income. Taken together, the effects of the cuts are great enough that many families will be unable to meet their monthly living expenses."

---

[12]I have derived these comparisons from a valuable study by the University of Chicago Center for the Study of Welfare Policy. This is a nonpartisan research organization whose director, the principal author of the study, was a ranking welfare administrator in the Nixon government.

THREE EXAMPLES OF BENEFICIARIES IN NEW YORK:
THE CURRENT SYSTEM vs ADMINISTRATION PROPOSALS

Monthly Benefits	Mrs. A(a nonearner) Current	Proposed	Mrs. B ($294 per month) Current	Proposed	Mrs. C ($457 per month) Current	Proposed
A.F.D.C.	$477	$477	$335	$274	$237	Zero
Earned income tax credit	None	None	40	40	30	30
Food stamps	65	41	35	17	30	68
Total income	542	518	704	625	754	555
Percentage of poverty line	92	88	119	106	128	94

The outlook is especially bleak for children. Inevitably they will share in their families' enforced general austerity. In addition, 700,000 youngsters will be dropped from a supplemental feeding program targeted at pregnant women and mothers with infants and preschool-age children. And as many as 8 million of the consumers of school lunches, 15 million in the bad old Carter days, may be rendered ineligible for these benefits.

As usual, the claim of minorities for the major share of suffering is strong. The 1980 census counted blacks as 12 percent of the American population. They are much heavier users of social services and benefits. Almost a third of food stamp and Medicaid enrollees and nearly a half of AFDC families are black. Overall the impact of administration budget strategy is racist in effect if not in intention. To complete a dreary accounting, blacks collect only 8 percent of Social Security benefits and 9 percent of Medicare support. The safety net catches whites more readily than blacks or Hispanics.

In one of its more useful researches, the *New York Times* (September 13, 1981) compiled from official Washington statistical sources figures that demonstrate that a great many dollars destined for safety net protections drift toward lucky people out of range of the poverty line. Of the 31.3 million Social Security pensioners, as a large example, no less than a third enjoy income from other sources, which locates them among the nonpoor. Of the 4.6 million veterans and their survivors who cost the Veterans' Administration an annual $13.6 billion, 91.5 percent amass sufficient income from other sources to raise them securely above the poverty line. In unpleasing contrast, of the 25 million persons below that line, 60 percent either receive no benefits or no more than, for the time being, school lunches.

Just possibly, the unneedy profit so lavishly from the safety net that there is too little left to care for the famous, elusive "truly needy."

Under cover of popular cries for local control, glorification of work, national defense, and free markets, the Reagan Administration has been engaging in an exercise in inequitable redistribution. The winners are the affluent, the Sun Belt, the white, the adult, and the male. The losers are poor, young, resident in cold climates, black, and female. Particularly bad luck for anyone imprudent enough to combine several of these personal or geographic characteristics.

The budget cuts mask still another effect. They are well designed to enlarge the number of low-wage workers and increase the pressure of continuing high general unemployment upon the entire pay structure. Implicitly Reagan's domestic policy is anti-union.[13] Slow growth in union strongholds and rapid expansion in anti-union states to their south and west have already eroded union membership and influence. The new budget tilt away from urban assistance and toward the Pentagon will accelerate the decline of union power.

Reagan's message to the classes and masses is increasingly easy to comprehend. To the middle class, the reassurance, "You'll be all right, Jack"; to the rich, a hunting license to grow still wealthier. To the poor, the injunction to get off your butts and start working like the rest of us.

---

[13]As the administration's merciless response to the controllers' walkout should have convinced the most conservative of union leaders.

corporate lib

John S. R. Shad, the chairman of the Securities and Exchange Commission, today gave his blessing to the recent wave of corporate mergers and takeovers, echoing the general theme of the Reagan Administration that "bigness in business does not necessarily mean badness."

NEW YORK TIMES,
(July 14, 1981)

A few years ago, during the brief reign of Jimmy the Irresolute, I spent a weekend in the company of John Swearingen, then as now head man at Standard Oil of Indiana and its Amoco subsidiaries. Around him revolved thirty or forty vice-presidential satellites and lesser eminences. We convened in a pleasant lodge on the shores of a placid Wisconsin lake, a deductible business expense like the company jet that picked me up in Chicago. Food was free, plentiful, and fattening. Hard liquor was available around the clock, although in testimonial to the observant eye of the chief executive, restraint and decorum were the order of the day.

From time to time, large corporations invite suitably attired radicals of peaceable disposition to address conclaves of senior executives, possibly for the sake of variety, conceivably to display open-mindedness, and most likely out of simple curiosity. Such, on this occasion, was my mission.

Responsive to my mandate, I courteously informed my audience that big business in America was an enormously powerful and far from invariably benign influence upon politics, culture, and daily life. I expressed my conviction that what major corporations unite in seeking from presidents and Congresses, they usually get. I waxed especially warm upon the capacity of huge enterprises, present company distinctly included, to manipulate markets, eliminate small rivals, dominate suppliers, and play off against each other, for tax and other advantages, communities and local officials. In pursuit of profit, I charged, corporate America gave as little heed as it dared to the health and welfare of employees, customers, and the places in which they resided and labored.

When, as fortunately sometimes occurs, presidents and smaller political fry intervene against business to protect the public, it is usually when business overplays its hand and exaggerates even its great power. Rachel Carson's *Silent Spring* raised public consciousness on a broad range of environmental issues. Hooker Chemical Company's Love Canal dump, Firestone's misadventures with separating radial tires, the fatal troubles of a DC 10, and the inflammability of Pintos, are reminders among many others that corporate products and practices can be harmful to health and life itself.

I did try to make it clear that business managers acted not out of innate moral depravity but in accordance with their roles and incentives. Businessmen and women judge themselves and expect to be judged by superiors and stockholders strictly according to the criterion of profit. Factory managers win small praise, and still less often promotion, as a result of improved plant safety and cleaner ambient air, especially if they have spent money and diminished corporate net income to achieve these benefits. In their position, I'd probably behave no differently.

For me, if surely not for my auditors, it followed that large corporations were entities too powerful and potentially too dangerous to public health and safety to escape serious regulation.

Hence my complaint about Washington bureaucracy centered upon the unwise leniency of its supervision. Unabashedly, I spoke up for tougher standards and harsher fines and criminal sanctions applied to violators.

Businessmen listen to critics infinitely more courteously than do academics. There is always the possibility of co-opting them. Although my oil men heard me out, I noted that Mr. Swearingen was shifting ominously in his seat. I was not surprised that his was the opening salvo of an hour-long counterattack against my indictment. I had it all wrong. Far from wielding excessive power and influence, competitive companies like Standard Oil of Indiana could scarcely make an utterly legitimate business decision without virtually interminable obstruction from assorted Washington warriors against environmental damage, market concentration, and allegedly unsafe working conditions. In their foolish zeal to affirm the rights of women and minorities, clumsy regulators pried into the hiring and promotion practices of personnel departments doing their best to hire and advance the best-qualified individuals available—in the corporation's own best interests. With the eloquence of sincere conviction, Mr. Swearingen cast himself as a contemporary Gulliver tied down by miles of red tape wound about him by modern Lilliputians in the Environmental Protection Administration, the Department of Energy, the Occupational Safety and Health Administration, the Equal Employment Opportunity Commission, and the Office of Contract Compliance, among other bureaucratic afflictions.

I recall this mildly diverting experience for two reasons. John Swearingen and every other influential business leader I have encountered yearns for freedom of action, defines his own operations as intensely competitive, believes fervently in private enterprise, and passionately detests all government interference. Some interference, however, is worse than other varieties. This is the second reason for my anecdote. It is the so-called "new" regulation that arouses special passion—product safety, occupational health, air and water quality, and racial and sexual equality.

For the variation in emotional reaction there is excellent cause. Regulation of railroads began with the passage of the Interstate Commerce Act and the formation of the Interstate Commerce Commission in 1887. Older regulators of railroads, electric utilities, trucking, air travel, and telephone service readily lapsed into cozy arrangements with the industries they were charged with overseeing. To this day, major trucking firms resist deregulation out of fear that new rivals would speedily challenge their long-haul monopoly. With rare exceptions, state public service commissions do more for the Consolidated Edisons of the land than for their captive customers.

Regulation of public utilities has been economic. Its focus has been upon rates, reliability of service, and conditions of entry into the regulated industry. Service as a commissioner or a staff attorney trained one for lucrative employment in the industry. Excessive enforcement zeal by an engineer, accountant, or lawyer cast serious doubt on the quality of his judgment and disqualified him from financially rewarding private employment. Saints and altruists inflame themselves with passion for the public interest. They are precious fauna to be cherished. The rest of us are keenly aware on which side our bread is buttered.

The new regulation gained some of its inspiration from the enthusiasms of the 1960s when Charles Reich hit the best-seller charts with his celebration of the greening of America. But movement affections for the quality of life had historical precedents in the more progressive episodes of nineteenth and twentieth century political history. Possibly more to the point, the extravagances of the flower children found complements in the self-interest of sober, square, middle-class and working-class Americans worried about the carcinogens in products, workplaces, the atmosphere, and water.

Old-style regulation seldom ventured beyond amiable negotiation between accommodating commissioners and business pals, joined in resolution of a common problem: how best to cool the public down when rate increases were convenient. Since the 1960s, life has become more hazardous for regulators and their targets because the public and the media insist upon participating. Rich or poor, we all breathe and rely upon water at least as a mixer. In the good old days gone beyond recall, only zealots followed tedious hearings of state and regulatory bodies. In response to their readers' and viewers' concerns, the print and electronic media sniff suspiciously at the maneuvers even of their major advertisers. Greater devotion to the public interest hath no owner of a newspaper or TV channel.

Such intense scrutiny makes it difficult if not impossible for the corporate sector to co-opt the regulators, especially because contemporary regulation spreads across industry lines. Bad enough. Most infuriating of all, the new regulation costs money. Smokestack scrubbers, quality controllers, safety devices, air and water filters, outreach efforts to attract black and female job candidates, and better testing of new drugs: none of these is free.

No wonder then that American corporations have deployed elite law firms in mortal combat against the new regulators and done their ingenious best to delay, resist, and sabotage the enemy. It is a testimonial to the underfunded and legally outgunned regulators that they arouse so much consternation in corporate boardrooms.

The excessive legality written into new regulations and the long delays that surround formulation and promulgation can be blamed then only in part on the bad habits of paper-shuffling, memo-writing bureaucrats in Washington, far distant from the gritty details of the processes they seek to regulate. Corporate resistance to sensible regulation compels regulators to spell out in excruciating detail new standards for safety, noise, and air quality and tempts them into regulatory overkill—seeking more than the state of the art allows at costs inordinately large for the benefits likely to be registered. Moreover, regulatory programs often conflict. At the same time as the Environmental Protection Administration frowns on pesticides, the Department of Agriculture endorses them. EPA campaigns for clean air while the Department of Energy promotes coal, the dirtiest of energy sources. Academics complain about the regulations that surround federally funded research. Horror stories abound.[1]

It would be amazing if an occasional zealot did not poise himself to go overboard in pursuit of regulatory objectives and equally startling if no instances of poor judgment and outright ignorance could not be cited by critics. The low esteem in which government is held and the low salaries offered responsible administrators ensure that federal agencies recruit less than their share of human talent and that the corporate sector attracts most of the best and brightest alumni of business and law schools. Under the circumstances, Americans ought to be grateful that able people do find their way into the federal establishment.

There is a further point. In regulation as in other aspects of American society, the adversary mode is dominant. It is unlikely that the best regulations emerge from protracted trial by legal ordeal. At Harvard's Kennedy School, Steven Kelman has been making a valuable comparison of Swedish and American efforts to improve occupational safety and health.[2] Although Swedish employers and Swedish unions frequently differ, they also cooperate in needed research. When the Swedish government issues a new regulation, it is rarely challenged by the affected industry. Until recently, social democrats were the governing party. All the same, Swedish regulations were no more stringent than the American, and, ironically, enforcement procedures were considerably more lenient in Sweden than in the United States.

Which is only to say that if one of the parties to conflict behaves in a hostile and aggressive manner, this is likely to elicit

---

[1] See Alan Stone's "State and Market: Economic Regulation and the Great Productivity Debate" in *The Hidden Election: Politics and Economics in the 1980 Presidential Campaign* (New York: Pantheon Books, 1981), particularly pp. 249 ff.
[2] See his *Regulating America, Regulating Sweden,* (MIT Press, 1981).

conduct from opponents that mirrors these unattractive characteristics. Many of the complaints of the Swearingens represent self-inflicted wounds and avoidable costs.[3]

One of the reasons for their impact derives from a so-far-unmentioned objective of modern regulation: improvement of business ethics. Levels of toxicity in drugs and chemicals are boring to read about and difficult to interpret. But bribery, criminal fraud, tax evasion, and criminal violation of antitrust statutes are fun to read about and quite within the grasp of the layman. Consider the record. Of 1,043 major corporations recently surveyed,[4] 117—11 percent—were "entangled in at least one major delinquency" since 1970.

As anyone might have expected, the oil companies, awash in cash, were frequent offenders. Ashland Oil pleaded guilty to making an illegal political contribution of $100,000, was found guilty of fixing the price of resins, and again pleaded guilty in three instances of bid-rigging for Virginia highway construction contracts. Gulf Oil was caught four times: twice for illegal political gifts, once for bribing an IRS agent, and finally for fixing uranium prices.

The oil companies were not alone in disgrace. *Fortune* summarized Bethlehem Steel's criminal record in two sober, succinct paragraphs:

> . . . the company pleaded guilty to criminal activity over five years, 1972–76, but the government contended that the kickbacks had been going on for a much longer time. The purpose of the scheme was to bribe representatives of ship lines to steer repair work to Bethlehem's seven shipyards or to speed up payments of bills.
>
> Since 1961, according to the indictment, Bethlehem has been using a Swiss company . . . to launder the kickback money.

---

[3]Standard Oil Indiana, for example, will litigate through the courts items like a $25 EPA fine for inadequate safety protection of a gas pump on one of its properties.

[4]*Fortune,* vigilant guardian of corporate morality, conducted the study. See its issue of December 1, 1980, pp. 57 ff.

OFCI was a convenient conduit, for it had a worldwide network of agents who drummed up ship-repair business.

Contrary to proverbial wisdom, honesty frequently fails to impress decision makers as the best policy. Compliance with the strictures of new regulation is annoying, expensive, and results in sour notices from security analysts and the financial press. There is a better way than meek obedience: disarm the regulators. If it is politically impossible to repeal offensive statutes, amend them. If amendment is not feasible, reduce appropriations and rewrite offensive regulations in the Office of Management and Budget, where sympathetic friends are now abundant.

Best of all, and a favored Reagan maneuver, employ regulators appreciative of business needs and views, foxes to patrol chicken coops. The Interior Department has been the guardian of national parks and public lands and the major barrier to unrestricted oil and gas exploration, timber cutting, and recreational development within the federal domain. Answer: appoint as secretary James G. Watt, fresh from his role as hired legal gun for explorers, cutters, and developers. Has the Securities and Exchange Commission been mean to corporations that bribe purchasing agents or deal in their own securities to the financial advantage of principal officers? Transfer Stanley Sporkin, the frightfully effective SEC enforcement chief, to the CIA and install as chairman the understanding James Shad.

The best of agency heads needs help. The White House sent Mr. Watt a certain Robert L. Burford to administer the 470 million acres within the jurisdiction of Interior's Bureau of Land Management. As a Colorado state legislator, Mr. Burford had sponsored legislation to return public lands to state and private ownership. And if a president is annoyed by the pesky Council on Environmental Quality because of its cowardly reservations about the safety of nuclear power, it can enlist such reinforcement as James F. McAvoy, a nuclear power advocate, who, as Ohio's chief pollution officer, distinguished himself by crusading for *lower* air-quality standards, the better to increase the use of soft coal. So that he will not be lonely, add W. Ernest Minor who, as quoted by the *New York Times,*[5] thinks the pendulum has "swung too far toward the environmental protection side" and wishes compassionately to offer "industry a break to get this country moving again."

For many members of the business community, the Occupational Safety and Health Administration has been particularly infuriating. Help has arrived. OSHA's new leader, Thorne G. Auchter, is a former construction executive who shares their feeling. As a symbol of excellent intentions, he promptly ended health warnings to textile workers and suspended a series of regulations promulgated in the last days of the Carter Administration.

As with health and public lands, so also with business conduct. According to E. Pendleton James, the White House personnel director, all the current nonsense about ethics and financial disclosure echoes "Watergate hysteria." One way to spare the nation worry about corporate shenanigans is to tighten the Freedom of Information Act. Another is to repeal the 1978 statute which requires the attorney general to investigate possible crimes committed by employees of the executive branch from the president downward. A third is to eliminate record-keeping requirements under the Foreign Corrupt Practices Act. If an upstanding American executive, pillar of the Community Way at home, must in the line of business duty bribe an occasional Arab potentate, better that the public know nothing about the transaction.

Democrats simply do not understand the needs of business. Republicans do. Here, for example, are savings and loan institutions that have been losing money steadily because they locked themselves into long-term, low-interest mortgage loans at a time when they must pay a much higher price for deposits. A hard-hearted soul might shrug his shoulders and comment,

---

[5] July 3, 1981, pp. A 1 and A 18.

"Tough! Such is the price of bad business judgment. Bankers are not supposed to lend long and borrow short."

Out of solicitude for the truly needy, the administration reacted more constructively and compassionately. As head of the Federal Home Loan Bank which supervises the "thrifts" (as savings banks and savings and loan associations are concisely termed), the president nominated Richard T. Pratt, fresh out of the savings and loan industry. Acting as disinterestedly as his colleagues in the Reagan regime, Mr. Pratt almost immediately authorized issuance of variable rate mortgages eagerly sought by the banks. Thus, inspiringly, the risks of future fluctuations in interest rates were transferred from fragile banks to sturdy home purchasers.

II

For their headlong flight away from regulation of corporate negligence, fraud, and miscellaneous mischief, the Reagan mob are awash in justifications. After all, in the land of the partially free and the home of the occasionally brave, it is all very well to insist upon honest, arms-length negotiation between suppliers and purchasing agents. Elsewhere in the universe the highway to arms sales and construction contracts is paved with the gold of payoffs to greedy middlemen, generals, tribal chieftains, and bureaucrats strategically situated to grant or deny import licenses, building permits, and other vital documents. Namby-pamby Carter types deprived American corporations of profitable business they surely would have wrested from rivals if only they had been liberated to pursue local customs.

We all appreciate clean air and water. No bloated capitalist deliberately sets out to endanger the lives or damage the health of customers and employees. For one thing, the publicity is bad for sales. Still, in all things there is measure. Prudent men and women in and out of government should compare the costs of regulation with its potential benefits. Utopian requirements bankrupt sound enterprises, threaten jobs, stimulate inflation, and console foreign competitors in more sensible jurisdictions. If the Supreme Court had not decided otherwise, Reagan regulators would have been free to apply cost-benefit analysis to new and existing regulations. The technique sounds more sensible than it usually turns out to be. Regulatory costs are frequently exaggerated and benefits underestimated. Some of the latter are difficult to quantify and therefore likely to be neglected, among them gains in sheer amenity. Health benefits are particularly hard to calculate because they reveal themselves over years and decades in diminished incidence of cancer and respiratory ailments.

Critics of regulation assert that in too many instances regulators substitute their own judgments and prejudices for the decisions of the market. For years, the Food and Drug Administration, for example, has delayed licensing of new drugs, legally prescribed in other countries, out of reluctance to allow doctors and patients to perform their own comparisons of potential risks and rewards. On fragmentary or conflicting evidence, regulators have taken products off the market that turned out later to be harmless or no worse than their substitutes.

Even when a government agency tries to encourage competition, it makes a mess of the effort. The Department of Justice has traditionally intervened against many proposed corporate mergers on the ground that they tend to diminish competition. On the contrary, assert critics, mergers often allow two relatively weak enterprises to compete more effectively against stronger rivals. Enterprises often merge because they anticipate major economies of scale and better prospects of operating profitably in expanding world markets. Are relatively inexperienced government lawyers to sabotage informed business decisions by older, more experienced, and richer corporate leaders?

In still other instances, regulation affronts cherished American values. Perhaps affirmative action promoters mean well. Nevertheless, they do wrong whenever they compel universities to admit applicants less qualified than those they reject, and employers to hire anyone other than the most attractive of potential recruits. Compulsory busing properly outrages parents who purchased homes because they were close to neighborhood schools. Like white males, women, blacks, and Hispanics will prosper in a competitive, growing economy. For such an economy, busing and affirmative action are fools' substitutes.

When regulation cannot be avoided, then economists, not lawyers, should operate its administration with the objective of replicating as nearly as possible market operations. Thus, instead of setting cumbersome standards for the emission of pollutants into streams, the sensible tactic is to meter the discharges and impose rising fees, much in the manner of the household gas or electric meter. Precisely as it is in the home owner's financial interest to economize energy use, it is to the business enterprise's profit to diminish chargeable volumes of pollutants. Once all parties rationally accept that zero pollution is attainable only in heaven, the sensible issue becomes the cost of reducing the unpleasant side effects of productive activity. In the language of economic analysis, "A system of charges makes it profitable to clean up until the point where the marginal cost of further cleanup equals the charge, but unprofitable after that point."[6]

For many conservative opponents of government action, a clinching argument for deregulation is the same yearning for local control as operates to substitute block appropriations for categorical grants. If a state or city is so misguided as to opt for regulation, at least let the inevitable damage be confined to its own jurisdiction. The wiser inhabitants of saner communities

---

[6]See "Economists and the Environmental Muddle" by Steven Kelman in *The Public Interest,* Summer, 1981, p. 107. The author offers the inspiriting prospect that ". . . with the increased entry of economists into regulatory positions in the new administration, one suspects that advocates of economic incentive approaches in environmental policy in particular and regulatory policy in general may begin to make more headway in the future."

will benefit all the more from the self-inflicted wounds of their neighbors.[7]

III

It is well to remember why all these horrible regulations and legions of meddling bureaucrats achieved their existence. In each instance, Congress acted in the 1960s and early 1970s in response to public perceptions of danger and public conviction that state and local action was inadequate.

National action is indispensable because capital is mobile, and the only way large corporations can be dissuaded from shopping for locations where taxes are lower, unions weaker, and environmental regulation less annoying, is to strengthen the federal role in tax collection, administration of labor legislation, and definition of national safety and environmental standards. In the absence of a strong federal role, states, cities, and regions will continue to compete for new enterprises and strive to retain old ones—by dismantling regulatory efforts, starving social services, and reducing levies on corporate property and profits.

A recent Delaware caper illustrates the way state regulation tends to function. Governor Pierre S. Du Pont, a member of the Delaware family which has long dominated the state, "has been crisscrossing the contry shopping for large banks interested in increasing their profits."[8] To focus its maximizing impulses, Delaware thoughtfully enacted a statute "drafted in private over a period of six months by lawyers for two large New York banks, the Chase Manhattan Bank and J. P. Morgan & Company, without any written analysis by any Delaware official

---

[7]Few of us are completely consistent. In 1981, congressional Reaganauts did their best to deny federal housing funds to communities that deployed local control in the pernicious cause of rent control. The leader of this (unsuccessful) effort was the extremely conservative new junior senator from, of all places, New York, Al D'Amato.
[8]See the *New York Times,* March 17, 1981, p. 1.

involved." In conformity with a custom not limited to Delaware, "Many legislators say they did not read the 61-page bill before agreeing to sponsor it and did not understand the complicated measure before voting on it." None of their business.

At last, a bill of rights for banks. Their reward for relocating portions of their activities in Delaware will be "a wide range of credit powers, unavailable in most states." They will be allowed to "charge interest rates not subject to any legal ceiling, to raise interest rates retroactively, to charge variable interest rates, to levy unlimited fees for credit card usage and to foreclose on a home in the event of default for credit card debts."

And still more. The state promises to tax relocating banks that earn more than $30 million in a given year at a compassionate 2.7 percent rate. New York subjects their earnings to the cruelty of a 25.8 percent impost. By no particular irony, major New York banks have led efforts to shrink the city's budget, improve the productivity of municipal employees, and pare social and other services. These excellent corporate citizens should not be blamed by admirers of free markets for their endeavors to rig one of their own.

The dangers of administration sabotage of regulation are clear and apparent. Even according to conventional economic criteria, they cannot be justified. Conformity to environmental and other regulation has been properly expensive for business enterprises because they have been compelled to assume costs that previously had been involuntarily borne by individuals and communities. Air filters, redesign of dangerous equipment, and other improvements in factory conditions are substituted for the medical and hospital treatment formerly paid for either by individuals or communities. Regulation has transformed external costs into internal costs charged justly to the enterprises that generated them.

To the degree that the Reagan Administration succeeds in weakening regulatory agencies and modifying the standards they apply, these externalities will reappear. Yet again, victims of noxious chemicals and unsafe working conditions will be burdened with loss of income, large medical bills, and the prospect of partial or complete disability. Communities will endure the added costs of providing for the medically indigent and cleaning up after dirtier industrial operations. Inevitably, the relatively weak will fare worse than the strong. Powerful unions in steel, automobiles, and a very few additional industries will fight fiercely and effectively to retain existing safety protections. Weaker unions and unorganized workers, more than three-quarters of the labor force, will be unable successfully to resist alteration of working conditions injurious to their health and life expectancy.

Much in the manner of Delaware's blatant bribery of the banks, states will compete to dismantle their own regulations, especially in the Northeast and Midwest. National standards do more than restrain harmful conduct, they also allow socially concerned, enlightened business leaders to heed their conscience without fear of financial loss from the competition of more backward rivals.[9]

Civilized communities and intelligent partisans of business concluded long ago that the health of market capitalism requires steady government attention to the context within which profits are maximized. If, as Milton Friedman and his disciples have insisted, corporations ought to follow no imperative other than single-minded pursuit of profit, it is all the more urgent that government define clearly the legal limits of that search. Steel, paper, and aluminum mills stopped their use of air, water, and the landscape as dumps for untreated emissions and chemical wastes only after Congress made these actions breaches of law.

With just a few honorable exceptions, employers actively

---

[9]In the last century, John Stuart Mill made precisely this argument in favor of factory acts that regulated hours and working conditions for women and children. They were permissible departures from the general rule of laissez faire and freedom of individual contract because a few wilful employers could veto improvements generally desired by their colleagues, unless they were legally prevented from doing so.

sought to hire blacks and women after, not before, the civil rights legislation of the 1960s. In the South, blacks became mayors, state legislators, and sheriffs in the wake of a national Voting Rights Act which compelled reluctant states and communities to permit blacks to register and vote.

Hesitantly, unevenly, and incompletely, all three branches of government have edged toward substitution of *caveat vendor* for *caveat emptor*. In the complex universe of synthetic materials and processed foods, sellers are infinitely better situated to identify and eliminate hazards than are the customers. A similar disparity in bargaining situation characterizes environmental action. The prosperity of many communities frequently depends upon the presence of a single, major employer. That employer quite often is a huge national or multinational corporation able to shop in numerous political jurisdictions for the most lucrative combination of tax concessions, zoning variances, and pollution standards.

Even a large city is no match for a corporate giant. In the summer of 1981, the defeated and embittered residents of Poletown, a Detroit working-class neighborhood, watched their homes and church crumble with the swings of wrecking balls. General Motors had graciously promised to open an assembly plant within municipal limits, if local authorities exercised, on the corporation's behalf, the public right of eminent domain to acquire a suitable site and turn it over to General Motors.

Blackmail? As a one-industry town, Detroit has suffered most from the troubles of the domestic automobile industry. The lure of several thousand new jobs sufficed to destroy a cohesive ethnic enclave. After all, General Motors could have decided to erect its new facility in a cornfield. On standard maximizing assumptions, it made no sense to embrace a "brownfield" alternative unless the politicians made it worthwhile for the corporate planners.

Deregulation promises a twelve-month open season for predatory business behavior. In its initial year of power, the White House symbolized its affection for corporate carnivores by casting the single negative vote in the World Health Organization against an advisory code applicable to the hawking of infant formula by Nestlé and other food conglomerates. *Caveat emptor* is a bitter joke on illiterate Third World mothers sweet-talked by sales personnel decked out in white coats.

The benign face of capitalism has been justly celebrated. For two centuries, competitive markets have promoted growth and efficiency, and widened the vocational and consuming choices of most men and women. The other side of capitalism is less attractive. As Adam Smith sharply emphasized, businessmen aspire to monopoly, not competition. In our time, mergers increase average corporate size and limit rivalry. Crowds do not collude, rig markets, and set prices. Small groups can and do. Bigness *is* badness because bigness narrows the scope of competitive behavior.

Their organizational responsibilities, reinforced by the best of economic advice, impel business managers to cut costs, the better to enlarge profits. The designer of a new car does not intend homicide when he shaves a fraction of an inch off a metal shield or locates the gasoline tank in a position more vulnerable to a crash. When they were compelled to do so by force of law, automobile manufacturers incorporated in product planning considerations of safety, fuel economy, and environmental impact. As these mandatory legal requirements are relaxed, they will diminish their attention to such objectives.

As to their current behavior, the Reagan Administration is gripped by a nostalgia for a world of unregulated competition that existed only in the utopias of economists. The completely predictable results of the deregulation crusade include reversal of limited progress toward parity by women and minorities, resegregation of many school systems, grave damage to public and worker health, and, most ironic of all, less competition and more monopoly.

the
monetary cure

To achieve the goals of the administration's economic program, consistent monetary policy must be applied. Thus, it is expected that the rate of money and credit growth will be brought down to levels consistent with noninflationary expansion of the economy.

AMERICA'S NEW BEGINNING:
A PROGRAM FOR ECONOMIC RECOVERY,
February 18, 1981

If "consistent monetary policy" fails, then administration hopes to avoid recession, check inflation, and accelerate growth will collapse. The White House gamble on the theories shortly to be examined will spell success or failure for Reagan domestic policy. Thus far, the major consequence of "consistent monetary policy" has been the painful 1981–1982 recession. October 1981 is justly celebrated as the month the economy fell off a cliff.

What, to start at the beginning, is money? Historically it appears to be something that other people, preferably all other people, will routinely accept in payment for things of value in their possession. For much of modern history, until the late eighteenth century, gold and silver were money. In the following century, paper money gradually supplanted precious metal, partly because gold and silver were scarce and the volume of transactions to be financed growing steadily, but also because governments linked paper to gold and silver by guaranteeing that paper currency could be traded for gold and silver upon request. Before 1933, in my distant youth, fond relatives frequently gave $5 and $10 gold pieces as birthday gifts. To be off the gold standard as for nearly half a century the world has been, is to make a dollar worth what it will buy in a store instead of some fixed weight of gold.

The distance between "money" and gold has lengthened as the varieties of money have become more numerous. Most Americans pay their bills with checks drawn on accounts in commercial banks and, in recent years, savings institutions. The writer of a check promises that its recipient can trade it for paper money. But by now most people have stepped even further away from currency. They use credit cards. Each time a bit of plastic is accepted by a department store, travel agent, restaurant, or service station, the seller (or the credit card computer) expresses his or its confidence that in the background lurks a check on a deposit large enough to cover the cost of the purchase, and behind the check the assurance of paper money.

A credit card is a promise that a valid check will at an appropriate date be written. As in former days, paper money traded for gold, so now one piece of paper, a check, exchanges for other pieces of paper, $20, $50, and, in the right company, $100 bills.

As sophisticated consumers have mastered the uses of credit cards and checking accounts, paper money has diminished to a mere 10 percent of the national money supply. The bulk of that aggregate consists of demand deposits—the amounts in individual and corporate checking balances. Twenty or even ten years ago, it was comparatively easy to define money: it was paper money plus demand deposits—"M 1" if you wanted to dazzle friends with your technical vocabulary. Ingenious souls in the financial world have expanded the definition. Thrift institutions advertise NOW[1] accounts which pay interest *and* allow checks to be written, unlike conventional savings accounts which pay interest but provide no checking services and checking accounts in commercial banks which earn no interest. At no risk, savers can turn idle deposits into active balances that are counted as additions to the money supply. Just to complicate matters further, the popular money market funds frequently offer check-writing privileges.

In the buzzing confusion of the markets for financial services, there is a traffic cop, the seven members of the Board of Governors of the Federal Reserve System, known to one and all as the "Fed." The six men and one woman who currently serve as governors are appointed by presidents for fourteen-year terms. James Earl Carter appointed four members of the present group including its chairman Paul A. Volcker.

Like the Bank of England and other European central banks, the Fed operates as a controller of the amount of money generated. It prints paper currency at the request of the commercial banks who are its clients. This is the smaller and easier portion of its regulatory responsibility.

The harder and larger task is monitoring of the quantity of checking deposits and their cousins, the NOW accounts. The Fed has its methods. It can vary reserve requirements. These are the percentages of deposits that commercial banks must hold idle in their vaults or on deposit in the nearest Federal Reserve Bank. The higher the reserve requirement the smaller is the fraction of deposits that can be loaned. Any bank that desires to lend more than its reserves allow can enlarge those reserves by borrowing from other banks or the Fed itself. The price of a Fed loan is the discount rate, a second weapon in the central bank armory. When the Fed raises it, banks are put on notice that funds are becoming more expensive, and even more menacingly that the Fed doesn't really approve of all the credit

---

[1] The acronym stands for Negotiable Order of Withdrawal, indistinguishable in function from a check drawn on an account in a commercial bank.

deals recently negotiated. When banks borrow from each other, the fee paid is termed the "federal funds rate."

These effective weapons are complemented by the Fed's third and most potent tool of monetary management, open market purchases or sales of government securities. Whenever the Fed buys a government security, some person, corporation, or other legal entity receives a Federal Reserve check which, upon deposit in a checking account, adds to the supply of money by its face value. Symmetrically, a Federal Reserve *sale* of a government obligation will shrink the money supply and limit bank lending capacity.

On the whole, central bankers rely heavily upon open market policy because it is most flexible and secretive. Only some months later do students of financial markets realize that the Fed had quietly decided either to increase or decrease the lending capacity of the banking system. The Fed can always enlist purchasers by the same technique competitive supermarkets deploy: cut prices and offer propositions too good to be rejected. Thus, a government bond merchandised by the Fed at a 5 percent discount from the price engraved on the certificate will continue to pay any owner the sum of money to which the federal government committed itself on that certificate. It is incontestably sweeter to collect $100 annual interest on a bond acquired at $950 than on an otherwise identical security priced at $1,000. On the latter, the "yield" is 10 percent, on the former 10.53 percent.

Here the plot thickens. If the Fed pays 10.53 percent on some pieces of paper, no one will disgorge sums of money for other bonds whose yields are lower, after suitable adjustment for the diverse risk premiums attached to state, municipal, and corporate notes and bonds. This is to say that the Fed possesses the power to push bond prices down to the point where they afford potential purchasers interest rates, "yields," as high as those offered by the Fed.

In principle, then, it might seem that the Fed can decide, according to its taste, the size of the American money supply and the rate at which it increases. There are complications. One of them is the mounting influence of the money market funds mentioned earlier. Small savers have learned that keeping money in savings accounts at 5 1/2 percent interest is a mug's game when inflation bubbles at twice that figure. Like rich folks, they have learned how to convert idle deposits in thrift accounts uncounted as part of the money supply into holdings of money market funds which are so counted. Consequently, the money supply is not entirely responsive to the Fed's manipulations. It is also influenced by the ebbs and flows of savings deposits out of and into small accounts.

The Fed has other difficulties, pre-eminent among them the mysterious Eurodollar market. Sloshing about in European banks are approximately one trillion dollars created by the sale of American merchandise and services to European customers. Nobody effectively regulates Eurodollars and for some American borrowers they amount to a convenient alternative source of funds at times when the Federal Reserve makes domestic funds scarce. As a practical matter, the Eurodollar fix is available only to money managers in large multinational corporations, certainly not to small businesses, suburban developers, installment buyers of automobiles, or newlyweds seeking mortgages they can afford.

As the Eurodollar market makes plain, credit stringency afflicts some borrowers far more acutely than others. Among the largest and neediest of debtors are cities, states, and the federal government itself, the last almost invariably in deficit. One of the reasons why the Reagan Administration does not so much as forecast balance in the federal accounts before 1984 is the existing interest burden upon an accumulated national debt which, in the autumn of 1981, crossed the trillion-dollar mark. An increase of even a single percentage point in the average interest rate paid on that debt enlarges the federal deficit by ten billion dollars. In other words, the Fed's acceptance, rather its promotion, of higher interest rates to check borrowing and calm inflation, will aggravate the problems of the budget balancers.

Interest rates are a blunt tool of economic policy. Yank them high enough for enough months or years, and all borrowers, the federal government alone excepted,[2] will be discouraged, but some much sooner than others. As rates escalate, the burden of interest is far heavier upon home buyers, purchasers of cars and appliances on the never-never (as our British cousins expressively describe installment credit), small enterprises, and cities and states than it is on giant corporations and the federal government. At some price, the latter, invariably, can raise needed funds.[3]

The monetary controllers since the end of World War II have hesitated to make full use of monetary weapons. They are aware of the inequities they inflict and fear that any severe credit crunch would create massive unemployment and deep recession, the precise complaints European heads of state brought in their baggage to the Ottawa economic summit in the summer of 1981, and poured into the unsympathetic ears of President Reagan.[4]

---

[2]Constitutionally the federal accounts need never balance. Endowed by the framers of the Constitution with the privilege of emitting money, the White House and Congress can finance deficits with new borrowing from the public, or, if need be, from the Federal Reserve System. States and cities are less favored. Their access to credit is constrained by state constitutions and even more by the skepticism of financial markets. Punitive interest rates compel cities and states to reduce public services, instead of raising taxes, to finance interest on the sort of borrowing for capital projects they are legally able to seek.

[3]On July 21, 1981, as it happened, the Treasury paid 15.56 percent interest on three-month Treasury bills, up a full percentage point from the preceding Monday auction. Since the federal government can pay its bills in money that it legally creates, the Treasury can always attract funds at some price.

[4]Money markets are internationally linked. If New York interest rates rise, before very long they will move sympathetically in the same direction in London, Frankfurt, Amsterdam, and Zurich. Unless interest rates in major financial markets move toward equality, investors and speculators will sell francs, marks, gilders, and pounds for dollars, depress the value in dollars of these currencies, raise that of the dollar, and increase the cost of OPEC oil and other dollar-denominated imports to their own citizens.

II

In any case, during the 1950s and 1960s economic success and steady, noninflationary growth did not seem to require draconian monetary action. The money managers steered a generally successful middle course between inflationary booms and politically damaging recessions. Moreover, although monetary policy never ceased to be important, the Keynesians who operated the levers of economic management stressed the fiscal implements of tax and expenditure variations.

For reasons conducive to much controversy among experts, both monetary and fiscal devices worked less efficaciously than they had in the 1950s and 1960s. For one thing, exogenous[5] events inflicted painful choices upon the Federal Reserve. When as in 1974 and 1979 oil prices quadruple, how should the seven experts at the head of the Fed respond? If they print additional currency and create large quantities of credit to accommodate enormous financial transfers to OPEC, this will inevitably impart unneeded impetus to inflation. The alternative, the straight and narrow track of financial rectitude, entails restriction of money and credit growth and accompanying gains against inflation. However, central bankers imbued with such virtue impose the costs of good character upon innocent victims—furloughed workers, doubled-up families, municipal employees, and legions of bankrupted small businessmen.

Until very recently, no democratic government, liberal or conservative, encouraged or ordered its central bank to pursue price stability at all costs. In the spring of 1979, Mrs. Thatcher

---

[5]An exogenous event is an occurrence unforeseen and therefore not accounted for by forecasters. Russian and Chinese crop failures are reflected in supermarket prices. In our own Midwest, drought has the same effect. An invasion of Mediterranean fruit flies in alliance with the political ambitions of Jerry Brown may suffice to interrupt a downward drift of food prices. Since 1973, OPEC has become a mass producer of exogenous happenings.

in England did embark on such a journey. At the start of 1981, Ronald Reagan joined her.

As long as Keynesian economic management produced generally satisfactory employment, growth, and employment consequences, monetarists were so many voices crying in the wildernesses of bank letters and academic journals. As Milton Friedman, spiritual father of monetarism in the United States, has acknowledged, the natural constituency of the Federal Reserve is the commercial banking community whose members are far more wired into interest rates and profits from loans than to stability in the pace of monetary growth. The individual Federal Reserve banks are actually owned by commercial banks in their territories and the Federal Reserve Open Market Committee always includes representatives of the Federal Reserve Bank of New York and other Federal Reserve banks.

The connection between ideas and interests tends to be tangled. In the instance of monetarism, the available evidence suggests that Milton Friedman acquired a constituency in the investment and financial community rather than that this community created a Milton Friedman. Wall Street monetarists are traders, investment bankers, and others who are sufficiently worried by pervasive inflation, even when its short-term effects benefit them, to give any doctrine a whirl which promises to restore stability to financial markets.[6]

Although most monetarists oppose a return to the gold standard,[7] monetarist prescriptions for a fixed rule to govern expansion of money and credit do evoke the certainties of a world that tied its currencies to gold. Between 1870 and 1914, the heyday of the gold standard, the Bank of England, on any occasion when its own citizens and foreigners were trading in more paper

[6]See Gerald Epstein's valuable "Domestic Stagflation and Monetary Policy: The Federal Reserve and the Hidden Election" in Ferguson and Rogers, *The Hidden Election*, p. 144.
[7]If the gold standard returned, major beneficiaries would be the Union of South Africa and the Soviet Union, the world's dominant gold producers.

pounds for gold than the other way around, would automatically tighten credit and push domestic interest rates upward. Higher interest earnings in Threadneedle Street, England's Wall Street, would attract investors in the United States, France, and elsewhere. They would buy English currency with gold and the drain on British gold reserves would first stop and then reverse itself. An influx of too much gold into England sent the opposite signal. An obedient central bank was then inclined to create more paper money, push interest rates downward, and discourage the movement of foreign funds into British stocks and bonds.

Gold no longer keeps the politicians and central bankers honest. The politicians first (and the central bankers a little later) harken to the distress of small businessmen, auto dealers, savings banks, builders, and municipal officials whose lives are darkened by the high interest rates that tight money invariably generates. If a central bank is to persevere in a policy costly to substantial segments of the corporate and financial community, it requires the legitimacy which is conferred either by the gold standard, probably not an immediate political possibility, or a plausible substitute for the automaticity of that standard when the world believed in it.

Monetarism seems to be the closest contemporary equivalent of the gold standard. It directs central bankers to exercise as little discretion, and to follow rules as fixed, as the managers of central banks in the pre–World War I era. As will be made clear shortly, monetarism as a technical doctrine has many weaknesses. It is even weaker as a political phenomenon. Commercial bankers are the monetarists' only substantial constituency. For them high interest rates swell their earnings. For practically all other businesses, they are a calamity.

The amorphous interests that support monetarism are the weakest elements in the Reagan coalition. If Mr. Reagan behaves rationally, he is most likely to detach himself from this doctrine and let the Fed know that the monetarist experiment should be drawn to a decent halt. As early as the autumn of

1981, there were signs that the administration was moving in precisely this direction, in response to the urging of supply-siders in and out of the administration, and many of the president's supporters in the business community.

Tempting as the allegation is, the monetarists who are, for the moment, in control of British and American affairs are *not* monsters, deaf to the entreaties of small children and their desperate mothers. They are men (and an occasional woman) in the grip of doctrine, that of Milton Friedman triumphant. It is a simple faith. Monetarists are sure that, although individual prices may and will rise and fall, price *levels* can shift upward or downward only if the money supply, however defined,[8] earlier moves in the same direction. The single qualification allowed concerns the rapidity with which money changes hands, the velocity of its circulation. But when velocity is stable, as monetarists assume it to be most of the time, then the escalation of the consumer price index must be the result of Federal Reserve action to enlarge the capacity of commercial banks to lend more to consumers and corporations.

Central bankers are no worse than the rest of us. Their intentions almost all the time are excellent. But their judgment is as fallible as that of any other human being. The "right" rate of interest is the rate arrived at in competitive financial markets by lenders and borrowers. For the impersonal decisions of markets, the judgments of central bankers are inferior substitutes.

Monetarists advise central bankers to be humble. Humility requires reliance upon markets, elimination of fallible human judgment, and adherence to fixed rules of management understood by all. If the Fed annually increases the money supply by the same percentage as GNP expands, say 3 percent as a long-term average, the reward of this policy will be, after an interval of adjustment, price stability. Then if OPEC does its thing yet

---

[8]To the pleasure of their opponents, monetarists quarrel among themselves with encouraging animus over exactly what money is and, therefore, what the Fed should be looking at in its attempts to define any policy, monetarist or otherwise.

another time, the public will spend more dollars on gasoline and heating oil but fewer dollars on everything else. Petroleum products will indeed rise in price but matching declines in other prices will keep price *levels* stable.

Once the Fed convinces savers and investors that it has found religion and given up sinful attempts to meddle with the volume of credit and the height of interest rates, dabblers in stocks and bonds will cease trying to second-guess an utterly predictable set of monetary managers. Instead they will expect supply and demand to determine interest rates much as the jostling of sellers and buyers sets prices in other markets. When investors sniff the spoor of lucrative opportunity, they will naturally strive to borrow the funds needed to exploit it. Larger demand for loanable funds raises interest rates and attracts additional savers. If, for reasons best known to themselves, people become thriftier and squirrel away larger fractions of take-home pay, then the resulting enlargement of savings will depress interest rates and attract new borrowers.

Human beings are rational. As additional information comes their way, they alter their expectations. If the Fed turns monetarist with sufficient resolution, it will generate public belief in stable prices and dispel apprehensions of continuous inflation. Once these fears vanish, lenders will cease adding inflation premiums to interest charges. Even if they delayed in so doing, borrowers would refuse to pay these premiums because they no longer could reasonably expect to repay their loans in cheaper dollars.

Labor relations would become simpler. Unions would not seek cost-of-living protection against inflation because neither they nor their members would expect prices to rise during the term of a new contract. Negotiators might then bargain over important issues of productivity and division of its rewards between owners and employees.

Implicit in the monetarist faith is the continuing power of competition. In the monetarist view, most markets in the United States are still competitive, in spite of government sabotage.[9] It may (to the uninstructed) seem cruel for the monetary authorities to do nothing about energy and food costs when exogenous events inflate their prices. There are times when true kindness requires a certain judicious short-term severity. Doctors who sicken at the sight of blood make poor surgeons. Central bankers who weep over the fate of home buyers, builders, and crumbling cities will never convince the world that they can stop inflation.

Societies, like individuals, pay a price for their follies. The United States and much of the rest of the industrialized world have indulged in a long inflationary binge and a protracted flirtation with Keynesian heresy. It will take time to convince the public that the Fed's union with monetarism is permanent and even longer perhaps to persuade investment managers that supply-side economics will open new opportunities for profitable investment and attract the savings needed to finance them.

Nothing is free. During 1981 interest rates hung stubbornly high in spite of the Reagan revolution in budgetary, tax, and monetary policy. Keen judges of investment markets think that throughout American economic history, savers have expected a real return of 3 or 4 percent as sufficient compensation for postponement of immediate spending. When the prime rate is 20 percent and the Treasury pays over 15 percent for loans that are perfectly safe, the market seems to be attaching an inflation premium of 16 or 17 percent.

Because, according to rational expectations theory, the market is always in some sense right, the continuation of high rates of interest must be interpreted as the collective judgment of savers and investors, securities sellers and buyers, that not enough information has yet become available to satisfy them that the Reagan and monetarist revolutions are irreversible. As

---

[9] I claim again the privilege of personal experience. On Dr. Friedman's widely viewed "Free to Choose" television series, I was a member of the panel of hecklers that heard Dr. Friedman claim that the *cause* of dangerously large corporations and unions was big government. Moral: sanforize government and the already exaggerated anticompetitive impact of other large units will correspondingly diminish.

soon as the important financial actors come to believe that the Keynesians, the fine tuners of the economy, are on their way out, and are convinced that the rest of the big spenders are gone for good, interest premiums will shrink toward zero and interest rates move toward single digits.

Monetarists counsel patience at home and abroad. Just as high American interest rates caused unemployment in Germany and France, their imminent decline will encourage recovery and noninflationary growth in Western Europe.

II

Will monetarism in league with competitive markets and rational conduct by savers and investors do the job? That job requires the makers of economic policy to nudge an economy afflicted by highly rational expectations of continued inflation onto a course of renewed economic growth without inflation—at a politically acceptable price. Ever looming before Washington's movers and shakers is the specter of Margaret Thatcher, a presence who floats in and out of any discussion of administration policy. She came to power in April 1979 armed with Reagan's assortment of intellectual odds and ends—animus against social programs, advocacy of lower taxes for the affluent, de-emphasis of government regulation of private business, and fervent monetarism.

Advocates of administration strategy resent the association of their president with Mrs. Thatcher.[10] Her strategy failed, they assert, because she failed to implement her principles. The Bank of England took nearly two years to effectively crunch down on monetary growth. Public spending as a proportion of British Gross National Product actually rose during that period. Even more contrary to her principles, Mrs. Thatcher sanctioned bailouts of failing corporations in both the public and the

---

[10]At the 1981 Ottawa economic summit meetings, Mr. Reagan took some pains not to be photographed standing next to Mrs. Thatcher. Like any veteran red hunter, our president is wary of guilt by association.

private sector. Moreover, the American economy is far stronger and more resilient than stagnating Great Britain.

Monetarism will succeed here because our central bankers have effectively slowed the growth of money and credit in the first months of the new administration. It will succeed above all because, unlike the British Conservatives, the American Republicans have demonstrated their capacity to slash government spending and reduce taxes according to supply-side principles. In the U.K., by contrast, marginal rates on incomes were reduced only slightly and other taxes raised by larger amounts. Mrs. Thatcher talked toughly to British unions of public workers but in instance after instance caved in to their inflationary demands. Here, the performance of her American colleague is even more inspiring. The destruction of PATCO, the air traffic controllers' union, signaled the antilabor attitude of the administration, and encouraged state and municipal as well as private employers to resist union demands.

When wages and fringe benefits rise at 9 to 10 percent annual rates as they did in 1980 and 1981, and productivity stalls at zero gain, the core or basic rate of inflation is also 9 to 10 percent. Sellers pass on to customers increases in labor costs. Higher prices set in motion cost-of-living escalators in union contracts and indexing mechanisms in Social Security and retirement benefits. If productivity were to spurt upward 4 or 5 percent, core inflation would be halved. If the investment boom materializes, such gains two, three, or four years later just might occur. In the meantime, the way to break into the wage–price spiral is to slow the rate either of wage improvement or price escalation.

In any conservative mind, the first is preferable. If sellers are compelled to absorb instead of pass on a portion of increases in labor costs, their profits will decline, the investment climate deteriorate, and the morale of executives plummet. If workers accept wage gains smaller than the inflation rates, profits will rise, and the animal spirits of investors bubble. PATCO provided the human sacrifices needed to terrify intimidated American unions into compliant behavior.

For reasons to be explored more fully in the next chapter, administration domestic policies are condemned to almost certain failure. Suffice it here to comment briefly on the specific weaknesses of monetarism. Some are technical—the sheer complexity of money, near-money, and monetary substitutes. It is far easier to state a simple rule for central bankers—3 percent more money each year and not a penny more—than it is to implement that rule. American savers shift resources from thrift accounts (non-money) to NOW accounts (money). European and Middle Eastern transfers of funds add or subtract from balances in large American money market banks. Multinational corporations that borrow in the Eurodollar market increase the American money supply whenever they transfer portions of these resources to American banks.

Quite often, in other words, the supply of money, according to any definition, changes for reasons quite different from Federal Reserve intentions. During the week ending August 5, 1981, for instance, the money supply went up by the unusually large sum of $5.1 billion. Why? During that week, Du Pont completed its acquisition of Conoco, a $7.57 billion transaction. As the *New York Times* explained the connection between the events, "Large loans to businesses can cause a money supply increase if some of the loan proceeds are put into a bank deposit that is counted in the money supply."[11]

Monetarism, beyond these grave technical weaknesses, is an approach to economic activity beset with internal contradictions. Monetarists seek to control inflation by techniques that will tend to raise business costs and thus add to inflationary pressures. Twenty percent prime rates add to inventory and other costs. They swell still further the price tags on new houses and rental units. For installment purchasers of automobiles,

---

[11]August 15, 1981, p. 29.

monthly payments are higher and the real price of the car correspondingly greater. Higher interest rates propel the consumer price index upward and nudge COLAs[12] and others indexing mechanisms.

Most factories operate most efficiently at 80 to 90 percent of capacity. The same high interest rates that stifled auto sales in 1981 actually raised per-unit costs on assembly lines working one instead of two shifts, three days instead of five.

Monetarists believe in free markets and government neutrality toward those who operate in them. But as a policy monetarism is anything but neutral. As we have seen, it discriminates against home buyers with moderate resources, small businesses, construction, appliances, and autos. It favors large borrowers. At the same time as major banks jostled each other to lend large sums to Du Pont, they were reducing credit lines for less puissant borrowers. Monetarism is equally unneutral in its impact upon public borrowers. High interest rates gravely complicate the troubles of older cities and states in the North and combine with defense contracting and other policies to favor ongoing boom in the Sun Belt and Rocky Mountain states.

Monetarists criticize central bankers who, on Keynesian principles, seek deliberately to influence interest rates and credit allocations among borrowers. At their most meddlesome, the Keynesians discriminated less among different categories of borrowers than the monetarists.

Perhaps I have been unfair. These may be no more than some unfortunate short-term costs of cold turkey withdrawal from the blundering interventionism of a generation of arrogant economists and misguided politicians. In the long run, monetarism will work, interest rates will subside, and the distortions and injustices of transition will be supplanted by the genuine neutrality of the money controllers.

Can we wait? We shall see.

---

[12]COLAs are the automatic wage adjustments to inflation written into some union contracts. The acronym stands for *c*ost *o*f *l*iving *a*llotment.

will it work?

The idea that's been established over the last ten years, that almost every service that someone might need in life ought to be provided, financed by the government as a matter of basic right, is wrong. We challenge that. We reject that notion.

DAVID STOCKMAN

If Wall Street were confident that this year's budget attitudes would prevail next summer, and the summer after that, the dissenters would cheer and buy bonds, inflation expectations would drop, and interest rates with them.

PETER G. PETERSON,
*Chairman of Lehman Brothers Kuhn Loeb Inc., former secretary of
commerce in the Nixon Administration.*

The impulses of mercenary nostalgia that inflame Reaganauts derive from basic misinterpretations of the American economy and its situation in world markets. The administration program is internally inconsistent, socially destabilizing, and politically divisive.

The legend of times past, the fairy tale of utopia regained, which persuaded 28 percent of adult Americans to install Ronald Reagan in the Oval Office, casts as heroes stalwart American businessmen, drenched in the virtues of their calling. They are energetic, efficient, competitive, and willing, nay, eager to risk their fortunes and sacred honor upon new products, novel ideas, and virgin markets.

Give them even now half a chance and they will sweep away upstart Germans and Japanese and restore the United States to its proper ranking among the superpowers—Number 1 industrially, commercially, politically, militarily, and morally.

What a contemptible crew the villains are! Big spenders on lazy people and the social workers paid to coddle them. Friends of whales, snail darters, golden eagles, redwoods, obscure birds and insects, and wilderness preserves impenetrable without the expensive paraphernalia of a safari. Universal nannies shamelessly avid to inflict their preferences in food, beverages, toys, clothing, and medications upon the public. Seekers after racial and sexual justice quite content to trample on the rights of white males. Economists and politicians who haven't had a new notion since John Maynard Keynes.

These enemies of enterprise, meddlers in the private affairs of free citizens, misbegotten children of the Great Society, have conspired to thwart our heroes.[1] They have imposed, out of envy, punitive taxes on successful people and corporations. With endless, misdirected ingenuity, they have enmeshed busy and productive managers in endless red tape, demanded libraries of unread reports, and engulfed corporate America in nonstop litigation. Overspending on the part of the federal establishment and clumsy financial management by the Federal Reserve have created an inflationary environment equally hostile to saving and investment. Bracket creep conscripts average wage earners into the company of those used to higher marginal tax rates. The federal government misuses the proceeds of inflation-swollen tax collections to maintain a large welfare population in permanent dependency.

---

[1] The conservative publicist Irving Kristol has applied the label the "New Class" to those who make their living in government as administrators of social programs and regulatory agencies, or in the academy and the media as teachers and expounders of bigger government as a way of life.

These self-inflicted wounds explain why the Russians out-strip us militarily. It is no wonder that the Japanese, fresh from their triumphs in automobiles and consumer electronics, threaten American dominion over computers and semiconductors.

Legends are inspiring distortions of reality. Japan is no supply-side paradise. Its leading corporations guarantee lifetime employment. Japanese managers avoid layoffs even during serious recessions. Government and industry cooperate closely. Credit is preferentially directed to growing industries and away from their stagnant brethren. The Japanese economy is informally planned by the alliance of business and government.

The German economy has had recent troubles but, until a year or so ago, its success was nearly as startling as the Japanese performance. Yet the Germans give unions a large voice in the management of industry. Douglas Fraser is a lone labor voice on the Chrysler Board of Directors. Codetermination in the German style has resulted in the enlistment of half the membership of corporate operating boards from representatives of workers.

Obviously the Germans and the Japanese have paid close attention to capital investment, efficiency, and the growth rate of their Gross National Product. In the constricted universe of American supply-siders, their success, far from confirming monomaniacal focus on assertedly strong connections between low taxes and powerful incentives to work and invest in competitive markets, very nearly contradicts central supply-side tenets. The Japanese model is an example of successful corporate planning. German codetermination should have, but evidently has not, hampered managerial autonomy while retarding growth, just as the generous structure of social benefits ought to have reduced work incentives and produced a generation of lazy wage earners. Supply-side theory is so simple-minded as make one wonder why reasonably intelligent people give it credence.

True enough, Russian addiction to overcentralized planning has made a mess of Soviet agriculture, housing, and consumer goods. True also that Eastern Bloc hunger for blue jeans, rock records, and other triumphs of American civilization humiliates Soviet leaders. All the same, Russian central planners have been frighteningly efficient about missiles, tanks, and military aircraft.

No matter. Our rivals in the world, friends as well as enemies, are foreigners. The American Way is the free enterprise way. From that certainty emanates prophecies that the economy will become dynamic as of yore as soon as tax and budget cuts, deregulation, and rigid monetarism register their impact upon the economy and the expectations of investors, consumers, and savers. Too bad that Mrs. Thatcher, subject possibly to the frailties of her sex, faltered in the application of truths she shared with Ronald Reagan. He will avoid her errors.

The Reagan vision is admirably simple. The world is sadly complicated. In politics and economics, sensible analysis tends to the complex, tentative, and ambiguous. Seldom if ever is it reducible to snappy one-liners. Since 1973's OPEC energy coup, all major industrial economies, Japan[2] alone excepted, have struggled with high rates of inflation and unemployment, singly or in tandem.

The days of wine and roses have ended. In the buoyant atmosphere of the long boom after World War II, stockholders, corporate managers, lawyers, doctors, blue-collar workers, even college teachers, came to anticipate dependable annual improvements in real income, only rarely and temporarily interrupted by recession. Prices behaved themselves and the mass unemployment of the grim 1930s receded into historical memory. Growth in Western Europe and the United States was

---

[2]Japan averted general economic malaise by a protracted export offensive which maintained its growth rate at the expense of the targets of export penetration, the United States and the members of the European Economic Community.

rapid enough to finance, without heavier taxes, improved social benefits and the completion, in Western Europe, of the welfare state.

In a celebrated essay of the 1950s, Daniel Bell hailed the "end of ideology." The ideology upon which he concentrated his interpretation was Marxism. Marxism was losing its influence because the class animosities upon which it feeds were visibly dissolving in the benign general prosperity of the postwar generation.[3] When economies grow, the emollient politics of something for everybody, narrows differences between contending political parties and renders comparatively similar liberal Conservatives like Harold Macmillan and Labor moderates like Hugh Gaitskell. However, as soon as growth slows or stalls, the nastier imperative of choosing among contending group claims substitutes the politics of either . . . or. In the United States presidents began to serve single terms, like Gerald Ford and Jimmy Carter, retire while still eligible for another term of office, like Lyndon Johnson, or depart abruptly after the fashion of Richard Nixon.

Democratic politics works most smoothly in an environment of moderate change. Events in the 1970s were immoderate. Massive transfers of tens of billions of dollars to OPEC abroad and domestic energy giants at home depressed mass purchasing power much in the fashion of a large tax increase on wages and salaries. Declining purchasing power translated quickly into rising unemployment. The sharp 1974–1975 recession in the United States accentuated the anguish of readjustment to energy frugality imposed upon the automobile industry and satellite rubber, plastics, glass, and steel allies.

To the consternation of economists, rising inflation accom-

---

[3]The joke will be upon Reaganauts if, as a consequence of the anti-union attitudes epitomized by the handling of the controllers, the loosening of restrictions on piecework at home, and diminished protection of union wages in federal construction, there is a revival of working-class militancy and the forging of alliances, new to the American labor movement, of workers and intellectuals. In 1981, Solidarity in Poland counted for more in the affairs of its country than the AFL-CIO could claim for itself in the United States.

panied slow growth and actual recession. The price of everything into which petroleum enters as a raw material rose—food, synthetic fabrics, plastics, electricity, and pharmaceuticals. Trying to sustain its welfare and defense commitments, the American government, and other governments, began to incur larger and larger deficits. Struggling to protect the incomes of members, unions extracted contract improvements far in excess of feasible gains in productivity. Equally intent on the preservation of profits and dividends, corporations passed wage increases along to the customers, usually with an added profit sweetener.

As wage earners experienced dissipation of wage improvements by inflation and bracket creep, union negotiators clamored for cost-of-living protection and larger pay hikes to make up for the impact of inflation during the terms of expiring contracts. These COLAs embedded inflation in the wage structure. Soon, all important economic and financial actors began to negotiate contracts, set the terms of loans, and bill customers on the assumption of endless inflation.

From this sea of troubles, there is no magical exit. I postpone to the next and final chapter detailed speculation about the sequels to supply-side economics. I shall there suggest that the best, though not necessarily most probable, response of democratic communities to the harder economic choices of this decade include at minimum a measure of democratic planning, public control of investment, achievement of consensus about the division of national product between owners and workers, and special labor market solutions for young workers and older ones displaced by the decline of older industries and regions. Such an experiment is under way in the socialist France of François Mitterand. If the British Labor Party resolves its internecine conflicts, it will, by 1984 at the latest, get the chance to conduct a similar venture. In my more sanguine moments, I envisage the sea change in American politics required to open the door to a nascent Democratic Left.

To return to current events, the Reagan interpretation of American economic pathology is all the more misguided because it neglects several additional American elements in the general crisis of market economies, each of them earlier identified. There is, first, the burdens of payment of the overdue bills of factory safety, product reliability, environmental protection and restoration, and racial and sexual discrimination. There is, second, the heavy burden, soon to become more staggering, of the military establishment, less on Gross National Product than upon scarce cadres of engineers, scientists, and technicians.

As Seymour Melman and others have warned, diversion of these specialists from the civilian sector explains much of the poor performance of American industry. In the words of Simon Ramo, a prominent high technology entrepreneur and adviser to President Reagan, "American technological development has been hurt, rather than helped, by our heavier investment in military technology as compared with other nations." According to Ramo's informed estimate, we may reach the stage of technological advance by the year 2000 that we could have attained two decades earlier if military research and development had been redirected to "those areas of science and technology promising the most economic progress."[4] If the Russians really are coming, the military program is too small. On any other assumption, it is excessive.

For true believers in the acres of diamonds to be harvested in Reaganland, a third American handicap is hardest of all to accept. It is the declining quality of American management, as relevantly measured in world markets and the showrooms and department stores of America. Increasingly, lavishly compensated American executives have diverted their efforts from research and product innovation to acquisitions, mergers, and marketing ploys, a tendency that has triggered belated alarm in business media and schools of business.

At the start of the present century, Thorstein Veblen memor-

---

[4]See the *Los Angeles Times,* August 11, 1981, pt. IV, p. 3.

ably interpreted capitalism as a contest between engineers and technicians hooked on mechanical efficiency, and entrepreneurs and legal and financial satellites caught up in financially enriching but socially useless manipulation of securities and markets. The manipulators, Veblen's business enterprisers, have been gaining ground. Veblen cited as a striking example of financial manipulation, J. P. Morgan's virtuosic creation of United States Steel, a merger of existing properties that added not a ton of smelting capacity but did earn a fat fee for the House of Morgan. Veblen, who by bad luck died just a few months before the 1929 stock market crash fulfilled his hopes and expectations of disaster, would probably have enjoyed nearly as much the merger frenzy of 1981.

Here is how one newsmagazine summarized the summer action:[5]

REWARDS FOR CORPORATE MARRIAGE BROKERS

Investment Banker	Deal	Fee (in millions)
Morgan Stanley	Shell Oil/Belridge Oil	$14.6
Salomon Brothers*	Elf-Acquitaine/Texasgulf	6.5
First Boston	Wheelabrator-Frye Pullman	6.0
Smith Barney	Fluor/St. Joe Minerals	3.5
E. F. Hutton	Kraft/Dart Industries	3.0
Lazard Freres	Tenneco/Southwestern Life	3.0
Lehman Brothers	Nabisco/Standard Brands	3.0
Goldman Sachs	Cooper Industries/Gardner Denver	2.0
Dillon, Read	RCA/CIT Financial	1.8

*Just to add to the joys of a new summer game, Philbro, a large commodity-trading, privately held corporation, swallowed up Salomon Brothers.

The pieces of paper shuffled with the practiced virtuosity of these investment bankers amply rewarded the stockholders and those who brought them together. At best, the odds were even that new and larger corporate units would be as efficient as their separate components.

---

[5]See *Newsweek,* July 27, 1981, p. 52.

II

The financial shell games of aging capitalism should not be confused with activities useful to human needs and enjoyment. It is not astonishing that the Reagan Administration views them benignly: the self-made millionaires who surround the president became rich by selling enterprises they had nurtured to larger corporations. Individually enriching opportunities can be socially and economically hurtful, but it is too much to expect the grateful beneficiaries of the first to recognize the probability of the second.[6]

No need to speculate upon the autobiographical sources of administration beliefs and prejudices. As an entirely objective matter, the policies that derive from them are individually and collectively calamitous. They are based upon distortions of reality that guarantee failure.

Let us count the reasons which support that last summary verdict, traveling down the Stockman agenda of budget cuts, defense commitments, tax reductions and tax favors, regulatory dismantlements, and monetarist financial management.

Fewer Social Benefits

As we had occasion earlier to observe, practical politics tempered ideological zeal when the budget cutters began to operate on New Deal and Great Society programs. The poor who voted least frequently for the president and lesser Republicans were handled with the roughness that they deserved. Early talk of

---

[6]An aura of anachronism does envelop true Reaganauts. Listen, for ripe example, to Charles Z. Wick, director of the International Communications Agency, explaining to the *New York Times* why the publicly luxurious life of his colleagues is an excellent public diversion: "During the Depression when people were selling applies and factories were still and guys were jumping out windows because they lost everything, people would go to the movies. They loved those glamour pictures showing people driving beautiful cars and women in beautiful gowns, showing that people were living the glamorous good life." See the *New York Times,* August 16, 1981, sec. 1, p. 30.

enlarging airport fees levied upon corporate and private planes and assessing yacht owners for the support of the Coast Guard quickly subsided. The middle class, whoever they are, were handled carefully, with one exception: It will be somewhat harder and probably more expensive to secure loans for the college education of their sons and daughters.

A foolish consistency, Ralph Waldo Emerson memorably observed, is the hobgoblin of small minds. Such consistency might have induced budget planners to tax the Social Security benefits of prosperous retirees and eliminate them entirely for the fortunate few in receipt of incomes from dividends, interest, and rents larger, say, than the national median for employed Americans. That notorious safety net protects a great many unneedy citizens.

For that matter, much of the budget slashing appears to be gratuitously cruel to vulnerable individuals and groups, less a carefully reasoned assessment of costs and benefits than an expression of distaste for inferior human beings. Elimination of the $122 minimum Social Security benefit, as a glaring case in point, would have reduced the income of men and women who during their working lives endured irregular employment and low wages. Curtailments of expenditures on school lunches and food stamps directed at elimination of duplicating benefits will damage precariously balanced budgets in low-income homes. Thwarted on this point by Congress, the White House even tried to reduce the percentage of earnings from work to be deducted from income in the determination of food stamp benefits.

In the Reagan Administration, compassion is as scarce as blacks and women in positions of prominence. However, quite apart from this lack of altruism, many of the budget changes are, in their own terms, ill conceived. They will save less money and stimulate, if anything, more welfare dependency. As earlier inspection revealed, whenever the cutoff point for eligibility for housing aid, Medicaid, or food stamps is lowered, notch dilemmas are accentuated. For a great many low-income families, cash welfare payments plus the supplements of food stamps, Medicaid, and public housing, are a financial package more attractive than a poorly paid job unenlarged by such additions. On only two unattractive hypotheses do these changes make sense. The first is sheerly punitive. More harassment, humiliating "workfare" requirements, and relaxation of federal checks on harsh local administration may be quite deliberately calculated to force adults on welfare into ill-paid work, legal or otherwise. The second emanates from the condescending estimate that the poor calculate less well than the rest of us. Unable to estimate accurately the enormous marginal tax rates imposed upon earnings, they will stupidly seek work on almost any terms. By any other assumption, it makes poor sense to arrange matters so that life on welfare is somewhat less intolerable than the sort of jobs likely to be available to welfare clients.

These disincentives to work effort, these additional discouragements to harassed welfare mothers genuinely eager to escape the humiliations of life on the dole, make equally poor budgetary sense. In the end, few dollars will be saved by reducing food stamp and school lunch funds if, as a result, unemployment benefits and welfare payments rise nearly as much. Employed Americans pay state and local taxes in addition to federal levies. If federal contributions to Medicaid are limited, the costs of caring for the medically indigent will be shifted to states and cities. If the taxpayers refuse to pay them, public health will deteriorate as untreated illness multiplies. In one fashion or another, sooner or later, interdependent societies either treat the mentally and physically ill promptly and properly or pay later for their neglect.

I have mingled conjecture and indignation in the last paragraph. In some instances, it is possible to quantify the consequences of administration budgetary strategy. A Stockman triumph was complete destruction of the CETA public job program at a 1981 saving of $1.2 billion and a 1983 boon to the Treasury of $3.6 billion. However, as much as 29 percent of the claimed 1981 saving will probably be offset by additional expenditures upon public assistance, food stamps, and unemployment insurance, as well as Treasury losses of payroll and income revenue.[7]

Taking dead aim at welfare dependency, overlapping benefits, and lax administration, the Office of Management and Budget has scored a bull's-eye on the working poor, the very people who merit the George Gilder Medal First Class for devotion to the work ethic. If, high on the administration's hidden agenda was fomentation of class warfare, few tactics would appear to be more appropriate.

Missiles and Men

One of several excellent reasons why, all during 1981, Wall Street's partisans of rational expectation theory were skeptical about Reagan prospects for victory in the war against inflation seems to have been their muted suspicion that the cold war against communism and international terrorism will cost more than is saved on social entitlements, will swell budget deficits far in excess of administration estimates, and delay indefinitely the march toward balance between spending and tax collections.

Notoriously, military procurement is the most wasteful portion of public spending. C-5 and C-141 transport planes routinely fly completely empty from California to the east coast where they are loaded for flights to Europe. If these planes were permanently stationed on the east coast, the annual fuel savings would amount to $40 million. Senior officers and Pentagon administrators use 300 enlisted personnel as servants at an annual cost of $1.6 million. The Republican Study Committee of the House of Representatives—there's a subversive group— concluded that the Air Force could save $1 billion by contenting itself with one instead of two complete computer systems at

---

[7]See *Effects of Eliminating Public Service Employment,* Congressional Budget Office, June 1981, p. xii.

each of its 105 bases. In Cleveland, the Navy Finance Center pays $915,000 each year to lease two computers available on the open market for $200,000. During the second half of 1980, the Pentagon investigated just over 7,000 instances of internal theft, bribery, and fraud. A mere forty-three of these episodes entailed $36 million in losses.

This is small stuff. The big bucks are in weapons systems. The Pentagon notoriously cannot or will not control their costs. In the fourth quarter of 1980 alone, estimated costs of forty-seven major weapons jumped an alarming $47.6 billion.[8]

Waste and inflation are close friends. In 1980, the Defense Science Board pegged at 20 percent inflation in weapons systems costs, twice the inflation rate of the economy at large. The board cited far more alarming leaps in the prices of important components: electrical conductors, up 170 percent; nonferrous metals, 86 percent; molybdenum, 267 percent; aircraft engines, 28 percent; and aircraft materials, 37 percent.[9] All these escalations occurred in the course of a single year.

The huge shift underway within the federal budget from civilian to military spending aggravates unemployment. Military spending is capital rather than labor intensive. According to Bureau of Labor Statistics econometric analyses, $1 billion expended on the MX missile might create 53,000 jobs, but the same sum directed toward solar energy or energy conservation would generate 65,000 jobs. Comparable results are 79,000 for mass transit and 120,000 for day care. As in the instance of CETA, this shift of emphasis within the budget will add to the troubles of the North and give an unneeded upward nudge to the unemployment statistics.

A larger defense sector requires more bodies to operate it. If Secretaries Haig and Weinberger, not to mention the president

---

[8]The Council on Economic Priorities collected these horror stories mostly from official sources. The last and most startling item was described in a Department of Defense study, *Selected Acquisition Report,* for the period ending December 31, 1980.
[9]See the *Washington Star,* January 21, 1981.

himself, sincerely believe the words they utter, the Soviet threat to American interests all over the world is grave and increasing. Nevertheless, the White House disavows any intention to revive compulsory military service. There are only two ways to staff the armed forces with a sufficient number of men and women. One is to create an extended period of deep recession and mass unemployment. The other involves vastly improving military pay and benefits. This approach is in itself inflationary and a source of additional price and wage pressures as the ripple effects of generous military compensation spread into the civilian sector.

In reaction, sensible or otherwise, to Soviet invasion of Afghanistan, President Carter, in the waning months of his term, sought to increase Pentagon spending in real terms by 3 percent annually and won painful agreement on the part of our European allies to enlarge their own military expenditures by the same figure. Reagan military planners judged 3 percent to be much too small. During the next five years, the administration plans to increase Pentagon appropriations (after inflation) by 7 percent each year. In 1981, military spending totaled $157.9 billion, 24.1 percent of federal outlays. By 1984, the Pentagon will be urged to spend $249.8 billion, 32.4 percent of the budget. Between 1981 and 1986 military expenditures will add up to a trillion dollars.[10]

The Pentagon encountered serious difficulty spending the modest $157.9 billion frugally allotted by the previous administration. Bottlenecks—shortages of critical materials, machine tools, and skilled technicians—already impede procurement and lengthen into years the progress from engineering blueprints to combat readiness of new weapons systems.

Those eager for the success of Reagan schemes can derive no comfort from the most recent historical parallels to this projected military buildup—Korea in the 1950s and Vietnam in the

---

[10]See *A Program for Economic Recovery,* Office of Management and Budget, February 18, 1981.

1960s. In the earlier episode, only effective wage and price controls kept inflation in check. Trying its best to conceal the scale of the Vietnam disaster, the Johnson Administration never asked Congress for similar controls. In their absence, between 1965 and 1966, wage increases accelerated on average from 2.3 to 6.6 percent. Consumer prices rose a trivial 1.3 percent in 1965 and nearly 4 percent the following year, at that time a disturbing figure.

The Vietnam inflation followed fifteen years of comparatively stable prices. The military plans of this administration must proceed within the context of an inflation which has endured for nearly a decade and a half, and generate expectations that prices will rise in the foreseeable future much as they have in the recent past.[11]

Many business leaders, quite happy about the cruelties inflicted on social funding, have been slowly realizing that investment in military procurement crowds out borrowers who seek funds to re-equip the auto and steel industry and preserve the precarious American edge in computers and semiconductors. By no means all the companies listed on the New York Stock Exchange are defense contractors. For the majority whose prosperity is linked to civilian purchases, military build-ups are bad news.

As is only right, I have saved the worst news for last, in part because it is somewhat speculative. Defense Secretary Caspar Weinberger asked his military advisers to outline the sort of industrial base necessary for doubling or tripling defense outlays, or, at the most, devoting half of GNP to military purposes, approximately the percentage of national product actually allocated to the armed services in 1944 and 1945 for the conduct of major wars in Europe and the Far East.[12] As the *Washington*

---

[11]For more on the historical parallels see the testimony of Dr. Robert A. Gough Jr. to the Senate Budget Committee, March 3, 1980. As the date indicates, this expert was concerned about the inflationary consequences of Carter's relatively modest 3 percent.

[12]See "Defense: Another Great Leap Forward" by Stephen S. Rosenfeld, *Washington Post,* July 24, 1981, p. A 13.

Post's defense specialist analyzed White House thinking, "We are coming into the presence of a new way of thinking about defense, the idea—unfamiliar since World War II—of a national-security commitment so unending and all-consuming as to subdue other economic and social priorities as though we were at war."

If all other elements of Reagan domestic policy were well conceived and internally consistent among themselves, if partisans of monetarism and rational expectations have it right, and if the president maintains his ascendancy over Congress and public opinion, the defense program all by itself will destroy any substantial prospect of reducing inflation, stimulating growth and productivity, and balancing the federal books. Perception of this danger led Budget Director Stockman to engage in his inconclusive duel with Defense Secretary Weinberger over adherence to the 7 percent annual growth targets in Pentagon funding and the massive $1.6 trillion to be spent by 1986 by the Pentagon. It is likely that this is a battle fated to continue during the entire Reagan span of office.

Christmas Presents for the Men Who Have Everything

As I may have been hinting, other portions of domestic policy are also ill suited to their own objectives. As it emerged from Congress, the tax legislation of 1981 contained a great many baubles for the rich folks in addition to the three-year slashes in personal income taxes for everybody. Nevertheless, good supply-siders could plausibly claim that much in the complex statute does encourage saving, investment, and more rapid growth. Since it is the affluent who save and invest most, kindlier tax treatment of dividends and capital gains, lower marginal rates on the high brackets, and virtual elimination of inheritance levies, all these boons and more, it is hoped, might contribute to the incentives of truly important Americans.

Set aside disloyal reminders that rich individuals and large corporations have been paying smaller and smaller percentages of their incomes and profits since the early 1960s. Ignore manifest corporate preferences for mergers, acquisitions, and speculation in commodities and currencies over the dull details of basic research and product development. Assume with the Gilders and Stockmans that ever lower taxes will stimulate added investment. Forget, if you can, the Pentagon's designs for a safer America. It remains as true as ever that in the short run (Kemp-Roth's three-year span of operation), across-the-board tax reductions are inflationary. One needn't be marinated in the wisdom of econometrics to apply common sense to the asserted connections between tax changes and new investment.

In the first place, even if affluent individuals do save most of their tax benefits, the remainder of America is likely to spend all or almost all of them simply to bring family budgets more nearly into balance. Moreover, investment in new and better machines, robots, assembly lines, computer controls, and factories (if it materializes) will, at the very earliest, translate into cheaper, higher quality, and more attractive consumer products several years from the moment the investment decisions are made. It goes without saying that the men and women who design new equipment and erect new buildings get paid every week or two even though the fruits of their skills take time to be harvested. Their spending in the meantime adds impetus to inflation generated by tax reductions.

There is a further consideration. When the moment at last arrives for the appearance of profuse quantities of salable merchandise, this yearned-for enlargement of supply will operate to dampen inflation only if productivity increases faster than the stream of wages and other incomes which parallels the process of production. Possible? Yes. Likely? No. In good years, productivity gains reach 4 percent. Recently, wages and salaries have been rising at more than twice that figure.

Administration tax policy is blind to the purposes and geographical location of the investment to be stimulated. Yet there is no reason to anticipate that such new investment as occurs will necessarily be at home, or if at home any contribution to the revitalizing of the American economy. Investors may continue to search for low-wage, anti-union environments in the rest of the world. Our affluent minority may continue to be attracted by real estate and oil drilling tax shelters, and speculative fliers in collectibles and precious metals. The aspirations of corporate leaders to bestride ever larger conglomerates may be facilitated by even better-financed takeover bids.

To assume that tax policy will reshape conduct, particularly when it rewards identically the enterprising and the slothful, the productive and the frivolous, is to leave the solid terrain of common experience and enter the gardens of fantasy. Tax cuts will add to inflationary pressure. They may stimulate some added investment in plan and equipment. They will certainly make the tax code, Jimmy Carter's "disgrace to the human race," even more outrageously inequitable than it already is.

Tax shelters will become more attractive. Since none of the tax benefits are targeted in productive directions, they are a massive payoff to large corporations and their wealthy shareholders without the slightest assurance of services to be rendered to the community.

Let Freedom Ring

Less than a month in office, the Reagan White House began to boast of its success in reversing previous regulatory priorities. On January 29, just a week after Inauguration Day, the president asked the heads of twelve cabinet departments and agencies to postpone effective dates of regulations previously slated to become effective before March 29 and to refrain from issuing new final regulations for sixty days.

As it began, so did the administration continue. The Department of Education withdrew new rules for bilingual instruction. These were designed to supply instruction in two languages for children whose language at home was other than English. The auto industry was granted a one-year delay for installation of passive restraints. The Department of Labor, in earlier, even Republican administrations as much an advocate of its constituency as the Department of Agriculture has been for farmers, withdrew an OSHA rule that would have required chemicals in workplaces to be labeled. As the press release ran, "Lower-cost means of assuring worker protection will be sought." The secretary of labor, a former New Jersey building contractor and Reagan activist, postponed indefinitely new rules under the Fair Labor Standards Act.

Here a touch of comic relief. The rules at issue concerned the salary level at which wage earners merited the dignity of executive classification. More than honor was at stake. Punchers of time clocks get time and a half for overtime. Executives do not. Who would have guessed that the executives of doubtful definition were managers and assistant managers of fast-food outlets and that, according to official estimate, degrading them to the status of ordinary "Big Mac" processors would have cost employers $50 million annually, "reduced employment opportunities," and raised the prices of junk foods?

Not to be outdone, the Department of Energy concluded that national energy efficiency standards for major household appliances should not be issued until a thorough review was completed, possibly never. For, in intonations of horror, its press release charged that "The 1980 proposal would require producers to redesign, by 1986, virtually all existing models of these appliances and to retool their production lines." Everyone would lose: "many small firms would probably be forced out of business. Consumers would face sharply higher purchase prices —about $500 million annually." Those damaged most, listen closely!, were certain to be low-income families "since the standards would prohibit continued production of the kinds of lower cost appliances they can afford."[13]

So it went. Wielding his own authority, President Reagan revoked Executive Order 12264 "which established a cumbersome, duplicative and burdensome regulatory policy regarding

---

[13] *New York Times,* February 15, 1981, p. A 3.

the export of some hazardous substances." In the nick of time, the president's alertness protected "American workers' jobs and prevented the disruption of production abroad where affected U.S. exports serve as vital material inputs."

These were dilutions of environmental, workplace, and product regulation. The Department of Justice presides over similar retreats in the administration of civil rights legislation, notably in the realms of school busing and affirmative action hiring and promotion. In the sights of the deregulators is another target, the 1977 Foreign Corrupt Practices act. Congress enacted this statute in the wake of a series of scandals involving major corporations. Not unreasonably, the act prohibits bribery, insists upon appropriate internal controls, and requires the keeping of honest books and records.

The Reagan ideologues flinch from outright repeal. They seek instead to weaken the act with a mildly worded, apparently innocuous amendment. The reporting standard now in effect covers payments to foreigners "in reasonable detail." Ah, to be a lawyer. For reasonable detail, the artful verbal substitution is "material." What is material? That depends. According to the testimony of a former SEC accountant, the Exxon Corporation's disbursement of some $50 million to Italian politicians[14] during the 1960s and 1970s would not be considered "material" for an organization on the scale of Exxon.

Legalistic booby traps apart, is there an argument for emulating the mores of corrupt customers and rivals? Hasn't the pursuit of unworldly integrity cost American firms contracts and American men and women jobs? These have been the expected arguments for weakening enforcement. The trouble has been in demonstrating that any damage actually has been done. In the three years since the act came into force, American exports have almost doubled. As Senator Proxmire has pointed out, bribery is bad business because when it is uncovered, hostile foreign politicians indulge themselves in costly reprisals. For-

---

[14]Including a number of Communists. Careful businessmen hedge their bets.

mer Treasury Secretary W. Michael Blumenthal denied that nonbribers, the straight arrows of the corporate universe, encountered significant competitive disadvantages. Prior to 1977, it is entertaining to note, Lockheed, among other major multinationals, deployed bribery as a competitive weapon against rivals, all of whom happened to be American.[15]

Bribery abroad, like lobbying at home, substitutes favoritism (at a suitable price) for efficiency. In the not very long run, both activities divert managerial energies from the pursuit of efficiency and technological improvement to the political and criminal arts. They constitute much of the problem of lagging domestic productivity, not elements of its solution.

Much the same judgment applies to erosion of domestic regulation. Efficient regulation, as was earlier demonstrated, imposes costs on those responsible for their creation, not upon captive workers, customers, and communities. It follows that the sums which enterprises save from deregulation will reappear as medical bills, higher local taxes, increased laundry and dry cleaning charges, and rising federal and state payments to disabled workers and their dependents.

Deregulation rewards the operators of inefficient, antiquated facilities and penalizes alert entrepreneurs who esteem decent working environments and high quality standards as important objectives. The jobs temporarily "saved" will be in declining industries that urgently require modernization.

For a time deregulation may continue to be politically attractive both to liberated corporations and blue-collar workers brainwashed into belief that their jobs will be saved. The administration temporarily at least can rely upon pervasive public impatience with bureaucracy and tempting allegations that the high costs of regulation add to inflation.

Before long, however, practical men and women will perceive

---

[15] I have relied upon the excellent documentation of Americans Concerned About Corporate Power, a public interest group sponsored by among others, Ralph Nader, John Kenneth Galbraith, Barry Commoner, and myself.

that laissez faire inadequately fulfills the public interest in the safety and reliability of air breathed, water drunk, products consumed, medications applied, cars driven, and appliances operated. In the middle of August 1981, Vice-President Bush's Task Force on Regulatory Relief added thirty additional regulations for review to an earlier list of sixty-one. Does the public really want more lead in gasoline, less testing of new pesticides before their introduction, lower safety standards for mobile homes, and less information about prescription drugs? These are likely consequences of promised (or threatened) review.

Of the thirty, several apply to women and minorities. Title IX of the Civil Rights Act of 1964 requires equal treatment of women's and men's athletic programs in schools and universities. The same portion of the act imposes responsibility upon employers for protecting women from sexual harassment. The act protects minorities as well as women from employment tests that unfairly discriminate against them. In the clubby, white male Reagan White House neither women nor minorities can anticipate much sympathy.[16] It remains to be seen how long policies that revive discrimination against a majority of the population will retain political acceptability.

Monetary Moralism

As John Kenneth Galbraith amiably described the dissonance between Reagan monetary nostrums and its tax and budget initiatives, "There are some contradictions in life and experience that can quite possibly be reconciled. The Israelites did manage to walk on dry land across the Red Sea. To combine a vigorous expansion of the economy with a policy of deliberately induced contraction, recession, and unemployment in

---

[16]One sign of changing times is revealed by the contrasting behavior of Griffin Bell, Carter's attorney general, and his successor, William French Smith. Bell, under public and presidential pressure, resigned from two all-male Georgia clubs. Smith retained membership in San Francisco's Bohemian Club, whose members are renowned for their habit, after imbibing too deeply, of urinating on trees.

order to control inflation will be more difficult."[17] The signals flashed from the ship of state are indeed confusing and contradictory. Three of them are invitations to an inflationary boom. Across-the-board reductions in personal income taxes carry the good news to merchandisers of autos, houses, and miscellaneous consumer goods that the customers will cease to sulk and start buying. By all means then, the second invitation, order up new factories and equipment, out of gratitude as well for the $40 billion annual depreciation bonus. And the strongest inflationary stimulus of all is embedded in the patriotic administration assurance that we will win a new armaments contest with the Soviets.

The Reagan mash note to American enterprise tells its leaders that they have new friends at the IRS and the regulatory agencies, many of whose former employees are now seeking more useful employment. The Pentagon purchasing agents will arrive on many corporate doorsteps, bright and early, pens poised over open checkbooks.

Not so fast. For tax cuts and Pentagon shopping sprees to spark genuine boom, a generous supply of new money and reasonably decent levels of interest rates are essential. When mortgages bear 18 percent interest tags,[18] all but the filthy rich drop out of the market for new or old houses. Although small and moderate sized enterprises create the bulk of new employment, they typically borrow funds at rates two or three points above the prime.[19] Steep rates discourage all categories of borrowing, but the heavier burden on smaller business further encourages existing unwholesome trends toward concentration

---

[17]See the *New York Times,* August 13, 1981, p. 30.

[18]In Canada, at the end of July 1981, the figure touched 20 percent, as the impact of American monetary policy resonated in a smaller and weaker economy tightly linked to its mammoth neighbor.

[19]The *New York Times* used to define the prime rate as the price paid by a bank's best customers. Early in 1981, close readers might have learned that the prime actually was the rate *around* which banks made loans.

of market power and adds to the scale of unemployment. Confronted by the high cost of new debt, many investors, including an occasional defense contractor, may prudently postpone new borrowing. Such action is particularly likely if, on either of two possible grounds, decision makers anticipate lower interest rates in the near future. Partisans of rational expectations began to forecast lower interest rates about the time Ronald Reagan took his oath of office. Their argument by now is familiar. As investors and savers rationally accept the firmness of Federal Reserve determination to drain inflation out of the American economy, the first group will be unwilling to pay and the second group will not insist on charging the inflation premiums built into the existing interest rate structure. The moral for business managers is plain. They will save a lot of money by waiting a bit before going to their banks or to the stock market for new funds.

The alternative interpretation of falling rates of interest is monetarist. Monetarists associate slower monetary growth with recession and accept its inevitability as a painful consequence of necessary economic therapy. Monetarists, probably more numerous and influential than rational expectation theorists, expect recession to be just as pervasive and deep as the constraints on growth of the supply of money credit that the Fed considers essential to diminish investor and consumer demand for money. As that demand shrinks, so in company with it will interest rates. The prophets of recession possess even stronger motives than the rational expecters to postpone plans for additional investment. In the atmosphere of severe contraction, excess capacity gets larger and the reasons for new investment smaller. In bad times, cash-rich corporations can absorb the assets of their feebler brethren at bargain prices. The cheapest way to acquire new capacity in preparation for eventual economic recovery often appears to be purchase of rivals in straitened circumstances.

When revival does begin, the Pentagon will yet again exert

its malignant influence. As weapons procurement accelerates, defense contractors will subtract a rising proportion of available investment funds. Their financial requirements will prop up interest rates, discourage civilian borrowing, and blight prospects of industrial modernization. The trade-offs convey an ominous message. Seven percent of projected military expenditures between 1981 and 1986 is the estimated cost of re-equipping the steel industry for effective global competition. A pair of B-1 bombers priced at $400 million can be exchanged for a rebuilt water supply system in Cleveland. Two nuclear-powered aircraft carriers, presumably a bargain at $5.8 billion, absorb resources capable of converting seventy-seven oil-burning power plants to coal, at a saving of 350,000 barrels of oil per day. The navy's F-18 fighter program, $34 billion before the inevitable cost overruns, diminishes the possibility of modernizing the American inventory of elderly machine tools.[20]

On the most cheerful and least plausible of suppositions, that recession will be brief and shallow, the threat of 7 percent annual growth in Pentagon allocations and far faster rates of acceleration in capital investment in defense plant and equipment, dampens hopes for productivity gains, faster growth, and diminished inflationary pressure.

From this trap of the Reagan economic managers' own design, there is the tiniest of escape hatches. It could be sprung open by unusual public behavior: a surge of thrift.[21] In earlier pages, I have questioned the probability of a break in the American habit of spending 95 cents out of any added dollar of take-home pay, particularly at the end of a period of stagnant or actually declining family income.

Nevertheless, it behooves any economist to be humble. To

---

[20] I have culled these examples from a useful inventory made by Seymour Melman. See "Looting the Means of Production," *New York Times,* July 26, 1981, p. E 21.

[21] As a patriot, I offer the White House a slogan to mobilize latent Calvinism: Save for a Stronger America. Moral majority alternative: Save to Slay Godless Communism.

paraphrase Winston Churchill on the personality and intellect of Clement Attlee, economists have a great deal to be humble about.[22] What just might persuade average Americans to save more? If they believe that inflation and interest rates will soon decline, it is sensible to get high interest rates for one's money while one can. Congress encouraged such sentiments by creating an "All Savers" certificate. If the public anticipates recession, its members may save, as a cushion against unemployment. Finally, apprehension about possible reductions in future Social Security benefits might stimulate (among the middle-aged and younger workers) higher savings to supplement retirement income.

Should the saving rate double, deposits in thrift institutions will swell, and new housing loans will be negotiated at declining rates. Sharing the savings bonanza, commercial banks will be in a position to make more loans at lower rates of interest. Major corporations now will be encouraged to float new stock and bond issues in renewed confidence that investors will snap them up. In this glorious financial climate, civilian and military producers will collect all the resources they need simultaneously to revitalize industry and fend off the Russians.

Alas, economics really is a dismal subject. If this scenario, against the odds, were enacted, its side effects would be predictably painful. People who save more, spend less. Just when mortgage money loosens, potential home buyers may retire from the market. Cheaper money for better auto assembly lines and more robots encourages little investment if the customers entertain themselves inspecting rising balances in passbooks. More than one road terminates in recession. A slump in consumer purchases, more than half the Gross National Product, is one of the broader avenues.

---

[22]The great man is reputed to have remarked, "Clement Attlee is a humble man with a great deal to be humble about." Right after V-E Day in 1945, the humble man defeated the great war leader and for six years conducted a Labor administration in Great Britain.

III

Up to this point I have tacitly assumed that, like its British soulmates, this administration will adhere resolutely to monetarist principle; the consequence of such fidelity is almost certain to be recession of unpredictable depth and duration.

Such fidelity is best not taken for granted. Mrs. Thatcher may not face her electorate until the spring of 1984. Our congressional jollities occur in alternate years. Nothing concentrates the intellect of a politician better than the imminent prospect of execution by indignant constituents. Even a president not up for re-election himself has party obligations. To fulfill them, a pleasant little boom just before an election is always a good idea much appreciated by the troops.

If inflation flares up with renewed ferocity and, to keep it company, layoffs spread through the economy, will Reaganauts keep the faith? Will they virtuously reject importunities from Detroit, thrift institutions, and other business supporters? Might not even the cherished military buildup be somewhat slowed? When Senate Majority Leader Howard Baker and House Minority Leader Robert Michel, while breakfasting with the president at the White House, anxiously convey the arithmetic of potential political loss in both houses of Congress, will Mr. Reagan offer nothing more nutritious in return than jelly beans?

The real question about the president concerns the relative attractions of ideology and power. Retention of the latter may well demand compromise, if not abandonment, of the former. For the supply-side, plus monetarism, plus rational expectations route to a better American future is rocky, twisting, and long. Persistence in monetarist restraint sooner or later guarantees the British rewards of deep recession and unemployment rates which echo those of the 1930s. In tandem with rearmament, monetarism threatens grave distortions of the economy. Starvation of civilian investment will stall modernization of older industries and handicap the high technology sector in its competition with Japanese rivals. Already acute regional disparities in growth rates will be accentuated. Defense and energy will generate localized booms in the Southwest and Mountain states. In much of the remainder of the economy, depression will imperil fragile recoveries in cities like Philadelphia and New York.

As some of this administration's own supporters will come to realize, monetarism's disguised agenda features some varieties of redistribution painful for them. The devastation of the Northeast and Midwest threatens the powerful unions which have in the past set wage and benefit standards for much of the labor force. A season of monetarism will compel union negotiators to make more and more concessions to management. For a decade American workers have been losing ground in comparison with other advanced industrial nations. In 1970 the average compensation (wages plus fringes) for American production workers in manufacturing was higher than in any of nine other affluent communities. Ten years later their colleagues were better paid in Belgium, Germany, the Netherlands, and Sweden, and almost as well rewarded in Canada, France, and Italy. In 1970 American wages were more than four times higher than those of Japan. By 1980 they were a mere 50 percent larger.[23]

Americans have been brought up to believe that they are the richest folks on earth. Mounting evidence challenges such complacency. If the admittedly tricky statistics of international income comparisons are to be believed, an alarming number of undeserving foreigners already enjoy standards of life superior to those of similarly skilled Americans. A monetarist siege will guarantee further deterioration of the American position in international league rankings.

Monetarism will widen existing disparities between rich

---

[23]These are Bureau of Labor Statistics data, cheerfully cited by the *Washington Post* (May 24, 1981, p. C 6) as good news for American exporters.

and poor. High unemployment, weaker unions, and localized boom in areas where unions are weakest, will tend, in conjunction with other Reagan policies, to diminish the share of wages in national income and correspondingly improve the relative situation of property owners and high-level managers.[24]

American business is no monolith. Small business, the recipient of few benefits from the administration's tax changes and crumbs from larger defense expenditures, is one of the major casualties of monetarism. Within the ranks of the affluent, some stockholders will fare better than others, according to type and location of activity.

For American politics, persistence in monetarism carries an ominous implication. The energy barons and the defense contractors have traditionally financed the far Right. The relatively civilized capitalists of the Northeast have frequently supported moderate Republicans. Political power follows the flow of wealth. The monetarist threat is, if possible, more serious as a political than an economic phenomenon. A tidal wave of funds for reactionaries might swamp not merely the remaining handful of congressional liberals, but also old-fashioned conservatives with lingering affections for civil liberties and civil rights and a frugal version of the welfare state.

With luck, I have outlined a nightmare. Possibly more likely is this sort of sequel. The president, disturbed by the pessimism and distress of his own constituency, might have a serious conversation with Fed chairman Paul Volcker in the course of which he conveys the amiable hint that salutary moderation in

---

[24]By lumping together wages and salaries, commonly cited statistics conceal differing trends in the two and particularly the resemblance and overlap between top executive compensation and income from property. Any self-respecting company officer of at least vice-presidential standing will insist upon a package of stock options, pension benefits, loans at concessionary rates of interest, and soothing severance pay, if things don't work out, all of which amounts to a property claim.

pursuit of sound principle sometimes counts as virtue.[25] It is unlikely that this news would be startling to Mr. Volcker, whose own constituency in the banking community had been letting him know in tones of mounting anguish that the way things were going not even Chase and Citibank would long be safe from the defaults of large borrowers. A man of conviction, but no fanatic, the chairman might breathe a sigh of relief and convey the good news to his six worried colleagues on the board of governors.

The Fed then proceeds to announce new and more generous targets for increase in the next quarter's money supply. Its change of course will not lack for heralds. Leonard Silk in the *New York Times* and Hobart Rowen in the *Washington Post* are sure to proclaim, with barely concealed pleasure, that the monetarist experiment has ingloriously flopped. In an editorial bordered in black, the *Wall Street Journal* will deplore the administration's lack of backbone. Milton Friedman will devote his *Newsweek* column to a wistful argument that just before the White House initialed its articles of surrender, signs of success were already visible to the acutely sighted. If only the president had not blinked, the nation would have soon enjoyed the benefits of his resolution. The editors of *Business Week* will no doubt remind their large audience that way back in the summer of 1980 they had prescribed, as the key to the reindustrialization of America, a social compact between business and labor, blessed in Washington.

For average citizens, more money means more hope. Among the still employed, declining interest rates make it easier to pay the monthly installments on new cars and even to contemplate acquisition of a new house with 10 percent mortgage money. Of course, these modest expectations will be blighted should it occur that interest rates refuse to decline, as the doctrine of

---

[25]To the consternation of true-blue monetarists, Treasury Secretary Donald Regan as early as the late summer of 1981 publicly advocated some easing of monetary restraint.

rational expectations predicts they would in such circumstances. If, however, more conventional analyses prove correct, the appearance of more money will diminish its price—the interest rate—just as a surfeit of avocados brings that delicacy within the reach of the rabble.

Monetary ease can be relied upon to stimulate both economic activity and Republican prospects. There the good news ends. Retreat from monetarism will simply return the Reagan Administration to the situation it confronted in January 1981, the combination that defeated Jimmy Carter, of too much inflation and unemployment, too little improvement in productivity, and no credible policy to turn pluses into minuses and minuses into pluses.

Its intellectual disarray may exceed that of its despised predecessor. President Carter did try to complement budgetary and monetary actions with pressure upon wages and prices. His misfortune was to embrace an excessively timid incomes policy. Reagan economic managers compound monetarist folly with equally vacuous opposition to any and all efforts to influence key price and wage settlements.

Retreat from monetarism may be in the direction of the far Right in the guise of a national security state. It may take the form of an abrupt shift of administration attitudes in the direction of national planning under corporate direction. Most desirable, and least likely, is a dramatic revival of the political Left. Our final chapter examines these alternatives.

when the
ball is over

For every tax break the White House offered the rich and powerful, the Democrats offered one of their own, sometimes two. They would give a marginal few dollars more to the less than well-to-do, but just as much to the rich. For the oil industry, the thrift banks, the nation's charities, a few thousand commodity dealers and those looking to duck estate taxes, there is no anxiety about the final vote on these bills. Heads or tails, they win.

NEW YORK TIMES,
July 26, 1981

"Liberal" Democrats indulged themselves in the craven behavior excoriated with unusual acerbity by the *New York Times* editorialist for reasons similar to those that in 1980 lost them the White House, the Senate, and effective control of the House of Representatives. To judge from their record, Jimmy Carter and congressional Democrats lacked sufficient attachment to the programs of the Great Society to confront the private business interests that blocked their efficient administration and expansion.

Between them the president and Congress arranged to keep none of the promises of the 1976 Democratic platform. Welfare was neither federalized nor reformed. No progress toward universal health coverage was made. In 1980, the White House quite deliberately plunged the economy into sharp recession and removed the curse of Herbert Hoover from the Republican opposition. Drinkers of three-martini lunches imperiled their livers at taxpayer expense in 1980 as in 1976. Blue-collar earnings continued drearily to decline. It was a black Democratic mayor in Detroit who destroyed a working-class community on behalf of General Motors and a white Democratic mayor in New York who showered tax abatements on needy retailers like Tiffany. Robert Garcia, representing Hispanics in the South Bronx, allied himself with Jack Kemp as sponsor of legislation to create "enterprise zones" in decaying urban neighborhoods. The scheme might or might not create new jobs. It was sure to reduce business taxes and diminish regulation of health and safety in workplaces.

Over and over again, Democrats proved that when compelled to choose between funds for social programs and benefits for the corporate sector, the poor lost and the affluent won. The Carter Administration brutally revealed the failure of liberal imagination and weakness of liberal nerve. Medicare, Medicaid, and the War on Poverty recruited majorities under two conditions. The prosperous had to be offered rewards as substantial as those addressed to their financial inferiors. In 1964 Lyndon Johnson astutely packaged general tax reductions with Great Society health, education, housing, and antipoverty innovations. Middle-class professionals discovered ample scope in their administration for their own talents and ambitions. Social workers, human resource specialists, psychologists, and economists did well out of doing good.

The second facilitating condition was assurance that none of this social tinkering would interfere with the operation of private markets. The doctors, hospitals, and health insurers who for so long resisted Medicare and Medicaid, came quickly to understand their mistake. They took care to divert large percentages of federal appropriations to their own financial benefit. It was the cozy alliance between health providers and Washington funders that alarmingly inflated federal contributions to these programs.

The experience suggests replacement of fee-for-service medical treatment and voluntary hospitals by a salaried health service and a one-class set of public hospitals. Although financially starved for many years, the British Health Service retains enough popularity to avert frontal assault by the Thatcher government. Liberals drew the wrong moral from American experience. They decided that universal health care was too expensive to contemplate precisely because limited care already cost too much and they lacked courage to oppose powerful private interests devoted to current market arrangements.

This failure of nerve and imagination was typical rather than exceptional. Although Congress late in 1978 did reluctantly enact a much diluted version of the Humphrey-Hawkins Balanced Growth and Full Employment Act, the measure became a dead letter the day Jimmy Carter affixed his equally reluctant signature to it.

Slow economic growth glaringly illuminated the narrow limits within which Democratic liberals were prepared to maneuver. Thus it occurred that by the end of the Carter Administration the major differences in Congress between Republicans and Democrats were rhetorical. Professions of concern for traditional Democratic constituencies of blue-collar workers, minorities, the urban poor, and the elderly sounded hollow to the ears of members of these groups under savage pressure from inflation, high interest rates, and persistent unemployment.

Nothing more cruelly exposed traditional liberalism's bankruptcy than the black comedy enacted in the summer of 1981. On July 29, as England indulged itself in the anachronism of a royal wedding, the House of Representatives voted 238 to 195 for the administration's three-year tax cut. Forty-eight Democrats deserted their party to endorse a delicious buffet of delicacies for potential heirs, investors in oil properties, stockholders, banks, large corporations, and collectors of capital gains.

Why not? Speaker Tip O'Neill and Ways and Means Chairman Rostenkowski had couched their appeals for party loyalty not on the lofty ground of principle but simply on the issue of party control of the political property. In a parody of populism, the best that Rostenkowski could claim for the Democratic alternative to Kemp-Roth was that it gave slightly larger tax relief to families with incomes below $50,000. Fifty thousand dollars happens to be two and a half times the median income of American families, hardly a definition of the truly needy. One does not bleed for a measure whose virtue is slightly kinder treatment of the moderately affluent than of the grossly rich. Such declarations of attachment to social justice merit the derision they receive. Accordingly, when large campaign contributors, mobilized by the smooth, computerized Reagan operation, demanded that Democrats rally to the banner of the president, the objects of that pressure might almost have been forgiven for their surrender.

Their choice between two dreadful pieces of legislation was facilitated by a clever mixture of administration threats and favors. Recalcitrants just might encounter well-financed primary opponents. If somehow they survived the preliminaries, they would surely encounter, in the main event, even more lavishly funded Republican opponents. If, on the other hand, they rose above party, they might have a free ride in the next election. Funds for opponents would be mysteriously scanty. Ronald Reagan would be engaged elsewhere than in campaigning for Republicans in their districts.

The president made some of his down payments in writing. A certain "Mr. English received a handwritten note from President Reagan, written on Camp David stationery, promising to veto any bill coming to his desk that would impose a special tax on the profits of natural gas producers."[1] Representative English's western Oklahoma district harbors, among other hard-

---

[1] See the *New York Times,* July 30, 1981, p. D 21.

working constituents, a substantial coterie of natural gas well operators.

So it went. One pathetic tale featured the vain attempt of a distinguished Georgia peanut farmer, active not so long ago in national politics, to persuade an obscure congressman from his own state to vote with the party. Mr. Bo Ginn did not long hesitate in choosing between a retired and an operating president. Along with seven other Georgia Democrats, he lined up with the Republicans. Two isolated Georgia loyalists cast sentimental ballots for Tip O'Neill.

Even when the political going was smoother, Democrats never neglected the corporate agenda. Business remains this society's dominant interest group. However, in times of Democratic glory, the party seemed able also to serve more vulnerable citizens. When Senate and House Democrats accepted the case for reduced social spending and quibbled only over the details, they gave up credible claim to possession of any alternative to Stockman's *A Program for Economic Recovery.*

Their consolation prize is small. In the absence of effective opposition, the administration's policies will enjoy the same clear-cut chance to succeed or fail as parliamentary systems usually, but presidential polities rarely, afford. Few excuses will be available for the architects of this experiment in reactionary politics when it unmistakably fails.

II

To assert that administration designs will be thwarted by their international inconsistencies is quite different from an unqualified indulgence in optimism. Individuals and groups of very different opinions and political wish lists cooperated in the first year of the Reagan era only because the White House kept their eyes focussed upon economic issues. When the news can no longer be concealed that supply-side economics accompanied and contradicted by monetarism turns the Carter presidency into a golden era of economic management, uneasy allies will be free to squabble in public—militarists, moral majoritarians, traditional Republicans, and old-fashioned conservatives.

For that matter, the managers of economic policy from the outset papered over grave differences among themselves. The pure supply-siders, David Stockman (in public though not in private utterance) and Jack Kemp, operated on the premise that several years of tax reduction were certain to regenerate the economy, and swiftly restore, even increase, briefly lost Treasury revenue. For supply-siders, budget cutting is optional but pure monetarism threatens to sabotage potential growth by starving investors of needed funds. The White House temporized by blessing both David Stockman and Paul Volcker. The good luck of legislative chronology permitted postponement of painful choice. That sluggish beast Congress completed tax action in late summer and postponed reductions in withholdings from paychecks until October 1, 1981. In the meantime, the Fed operated the only circus in town.[2]

Monetarists and supply-siders know the truth. The trouble is that truth for the monetarists involves salvation by recession, unemployment, business bankruptcy, and fairly protracted slow recovery. A more cheerful lot, supply-siders promise to cure inflation by enlarging output, improving productivity, and encouraging saving. To succeed, the supply-side prescription needs the aid of low interest rates and generous quantities of credit. Although there is no reason to believe that, under optimum conditions, supply-side confidence in the efficacy of tax incentives is justified, these incentives must surely fail when monetarists sabotage them.

Determined monetarism will always vanquish supply-side economics. The monetary screws, if sufficiently tightened, can

---

[2]Two prominent supply-siders jumped off the Reagan bandwagon in August. Both Jude Wanniski and Arthur B. Laffer attacked the administration for yielding to the monetarists. They predict that Reagan's program will founder in a collision between fiscal stimulation and Fed restraints on money growth. See *Business Week*, August 24, 1981, p. 78, for an account of their displeasure.

be relied upon to generate interest rates high enough to cool the ardor of the most enthusiastic investor and destroy the market for homes and automobiles. In the Reagan Administration, the supply-siders will get their chance only if the monetarists are expelled from the halls of the Federal Reserve.

Somewhat more probable is a shift to the agenda of the hard, moralistic, fundamentalist political right. Monetarists and supply-siders are not my favorite people, but their monomanias tend to protect the Republic from worse afflictions and their faith in competitive markets extends to the freedoms guaranteed by the Bill of Rights. The agenda of the Moral Majority and congressional allies like Senators Jesse Helms and James East threaten personal liberty. Their familiar little list emphasizes constitutional prohibition of abortion under any circumstances, compulsory school prayer, censorship of ideas as well as pornography, creationism in biology texts, and renewed quests for subversives.[3]

By themselves, the Moral Majoritarians almost surely do not command sufficient public support to advance much if any of their agenda through Congress. Frequently, however, they can count on the support of the potent national security establishment—the Pentagon, the intelligence community, defense contractors, energy conglomerates, and their powerful political friends. For those so minded, connections are readily traced between Soviet global aggression and American weakness perceived as a result of the disintegration of the family, humanistic takeovers in the public schools, radical subversion of the National Council of Churches, and liberal dominion over network news programs.

---

[3]On the last theme, one section of the intellectual community will probably offer valuable assistance. The neoconservatives in the *Commentary–Public Interest* coterie share many of the foreign policy attitudes of rightist journals like *Policy Review,* an organ of the Heritage Foundation, and *The Washington Review,* sponsored by the rather less feverish Georgetown University Center for the Study of Strategic and International Issues. Fear of Soviet aggression is neatly complemented by paranoia over Soviet moles burrowing in the CIA, the media, liberal think tanks, universities, and labor unions.

The Reagan Administration has enlarged the power and influence of the military-industrial-intelligence-energy complex far beyond Dwight Eisenhower's fears in his concluding message as president. Within the federal government, larger military budgets and smaller civilian appropriations shift the odds in favor of the Pentagon whenever OMB puts together a new budget. Events in the private sector echo changes in federal priorities. Defense industry becomes more important. The conservative states, in which defense contracts are concentrated, attract larger shares of new investment and migrants from the North.

CIA Director William Casey's publicly stated mission has been restoration of the "company's" élan, apparently by unleashing its dirty tricks operators[4] as in the good old days of the 1950s and 1960s when the CIA overthrew leftist governments and plotted the "expedient demise"[5] of inconvenient foreign potentates.

For the CIA 1981 was an excellent year. Congress relaxed its surveillance and plans are under way to amend the Freedom of Information Act to exempt the CIA from risk of occasional embarrassing revelations of previous malfeasance. By upholding withdrawal of Philip Agee's passport, the Supreme Court gave the CIA its sweetest victory. It is not essential to endorse Agee's campaign to expose CIA agents around the world to reject infringement of First Amendment liberties by a Supreme Court apparently angrier at Agee than concerned about the Constitution.

The energy industry also celebrated a banner year. It began with speedy removal of oil price controls, continued with congressional modification of the windfall profits tax on swollen

---

[4]In August 1981, *Newsweek* printed an account of an alleged CIA coup against Libya's unappealing strong man Colonel Khadafy. One can deplore the man without cheering the plot. Shortly afterwards American fighter planes shot down two Libyan jets sixty miles off the Libyan coast.

[5]The locution is Len Deighton's. *XPD*, the title of his latest thriller, is short for "expedient demise" and a delightful euphemism for the nasty word "assassination."

profits, and ended with promises of even better news in the near future. Residual controls over natural gas prices might soon be junked. Ascendant deregulators in OMB and Secretary Watt's Interior Department had already begun to relax environmental restrictions against exploration on public lands and in offshore tracts. OMB had reduced administration support for solar energy alternatives to fossil fuels. Although Mobil was thwarted in its takeover bid for Conoco, the Department of Justice had made it clear that it stood ready to approve almost any subsequent merger attempt by Mobil and its peers.

This administration has accelerated the steady shift of financial and political power from the Northeast and Midwest to the Southwest, Mountain states, and Far West. Thomas E. Dewey of New York was the last eastern Republican to run, though unsuccessfully, for the presidency. The year was 1948. Goldwater's defeat of Nelson Rockefeller in 1964 recorded the official demise of eastern Republicanism as the dominant voice of the party. In 1980 a little known, far right suburban Republican defeated the veteran liberal Jacob Javits in the primaries. Allegedly progressive New York Republicans dismissed the man who had represented them for nearly a quarter of a century. Eastern Republicans had apparently embraced the views of colleagues in other parts of the country.

After the redistricting compelled by the 1980 census, the right wing of both parties will be substantially strengthened. The Northeast and the industrial Midwest will lose seats in the House of Representatives to the conservative Sun Belt and Mountain states. As the president demonstrated in his budgetary and tax cut triumphs in 1981, the "boll weevil" caucus is at least as conservative as Republicans from the same region. In Texas, Louisiana, Georgia, and states of similar political disposition, politicians who, faithful to tradition, continue to call themselves Democrats, at least as long as committee and subcommittee chairmanships are available prizes, compete for corporate support with Republicans. The states of the Sun Belt have turned into single-party constituencies in which the attitudes, voting records, and sources of support of Democrats and Republicans are indistinguishable.

In the best of times, the national passion for civil liberties burns with an uncertain flame. During crises, the flame flickers dangerously. In the context of economic failure, the temptation will be powerful to rescue a faltering administration by a dramatic call to arms. Mr. Reagan, before he turned to politics, made an excellent living out of anti-Communist speeches on behalf of General Electric. Dominant figures in his administration have long records as foreign policy hardliners. Strewn about the geopolitical landscape are convenient symbols of creeping or lurching communism. The durable Fidel Castro continues to export sugar to the Soviet Union and subversion to Central America. Heroic Afghanistan stands as a bleeding reproach to the weakness of the Free World. Russian missiles threaten Western Europe, where disquieting neutralism spreads and raises the specter of self-Finlandization.[6]

The Soviets, whose national security state has been in full operation since the October Revolution, can be depended upon to cooperate with the more psychotic fantasies of American cold warriors. When, in a year or two or sooner, the confluence of economic calamity and reactionary politics requires new administration policies, it should be comparatively simple to concoct a grave international crisis.

On appropriate occasions, Ronald Reagan likes to compare himself and his New Beginning for America with Franklin Roosevelt and the New Deal. As the president fails to add, the New Deal, for all its innovations and reforms, alleviated but did not cure the mass unemployment that it inherited. On the eve of Pearl Harbor, unemployment was running at 14 percent and American Keynesians were speculating about the dangers of permanent stagnation. By ending unemployment, World War II empirically verified Keynes's definition of unemployment as a consequence of deficient aggregate demand. As the world

---

[6]A coinage of *Commentary*'s editor, Norman Podhoretz, a strident viewer with alarm.

knows, there is nothing like a major war to absorb as many unused resources and idle people as disordered economies can create.

The nuclear age has eliminated the possibility of direct conflict between superpowers, except by horrible accident. Nuclear exchanges create no winners. Superpowers must conduct their wars either through surrogates or in carefully limited spheres of influence. The Soviets could try to subdue the Afghans with no more than token reprisal from the United States. We operate with similar freedom in Central America and, less certainly, in Cuba. The price of unchallenged American handling of Castro may be tacit American acceptance of Soviet intervention, if not in Poland, in another restive East European satellite.

Armed clashes between huge ground forces on the World War II model are highly unlikely. With the possible exception of semicrazed defense intellectuals, no one believes that nuclear weapons would not be brought into play by the losing side in any NATO-Warsaw Pact confrontation on the north German plain. Only war game theorists think it possible that nuclear exchanges which begin with tactical, battlefield weapons would not speedily escalate to the exchange of intercontinental ballistic missiles.

It follows that the difficult, maybe impossible challenge for partisans of a national security state in a democracy is organization of public support for permanent crisis at a subnuclear level. Only perpetually simmering crisis can justify an occasional small war and permanent consignment of enormous resources to the fabrication of B-1 and stealth bombers, nuclear aircraft carriers and submarines, ever more intricate and expensive battle tanks, laser weapons, nerve gas laboratories, and military space stations.

A vastly expanded national security apparatus will not operate with only volunteer help, for there is simply no way to double or treble the size of the uniformed forces without enormous enlargement of pay and benefits. Quite possibly, even exceptionally large pecuniary bribes will fail to bid away from defense plants skilled workers and educated specialists essential to military efficiency.

For the stewards of a national security state, the politics of conscription is hazardous. At the start of the 1980s, scattered resistance to apparently innocuous draft registration measured the depth of antipathy to compulsory military service on the part of the young and their parents. During the Vietnam War, antiwar sentiment strikingly cooled after the Nixon Administration eliminated the draft.

It is possible that even endemic crisis will not reconcile a generation deeply opposed to restrictions upon the conduct of their personal lives to renewed conscription. As it may appear to crisis managers, the solution will imitate the Reagan handling of the controllers' walkout. Severe penalties for draft resistance, show trials of the least popular resisters, and accusations of subversion conveniently complement sedulously nurtured apprehensions about Soviet machinations in American higher education. The mellow voice levels and understated rhetoric popular in the White House and appropriate to the president's initial emphasis upon taxes and spending, ought not disguise basic attitudes. The president's major advisers share the sentiments he articulated for so long on the lecture circuit. Edwin Meese III, the president's closest adviser, a well-known friend of the police, has criticized the American Civil Liberties Union as a lobbyist for criminals. Secretary Haig's interpretation of the Constitution emerged in the last days of the Nixon Administration when, thwarted by Attorney General Elliott Richardson's refusal to fire Special Prosecutor Archibald Cox, he told him reproachfully that he was disobeying an order from his commander in chief.

Economic disorder and international crisis, genuine or contrived, could set the stage for the declaration of a national emergency which justifies suppression of normal civil liberties on grounds of internal security. After Pearl Harbor, Franklin Roosevelt penned up loyal Japanese-Americans, many born in this country, in concentration camps. It is sobering to recall that Supreme Court libertarians like William O. Douglas and Hugo Black endorsed this action. There's a precedent for a president who admires Franklin Roosevelt.

In the 1950s, Americans were lucky. Senator Joseph McCarthy, as much buffoon and alcoholic as ideologue, latched onto Red-hunting almost by accident, while casting about for a re-election issue. Respectable Republicans like Senator Robert Taft and President Eisenhower at times wielded him as a hammer against Democrats but ultimately discarded him when his behavior became too erratic to be useful. The 1950s were comparatively prosperous, American cities were calm, the American writ was respected in the world, and President Eisenhower himself sat more comfortably on golf carts than on white horses. Callous political operator that he was, Joe McCarthy ruined many careers, seriously damaged the State Department, and fastened onto government employers and defense contractors an enduring and offensive security and loyalty apparatus. Not bad for a politician who believed few of his own words and allegations.

Serious people staff the Reagan Administration. For many, if not most, Americans this is a financially difficult decade. In the outside world, mobs of Iranians hold American diplomats and a CIA operative or two hostage with impunity. The effort to rescue them collapses into technological shambles. Just ninety miles from the Florida coast, Castro sneers at his formerly mighty neighbor and dispatches troops to Angola as though it were Vietnam. Some of our experts appear to really believe that the Soviets are preparing themselves to conduct a thermonuclear war that they expect to win, so enfeebled are our weapons of reprisal.

The national security state is a nightmare that makes one hope that supply-side economics will succeed. Plutocracy is preferable to the repressions of the permanently mobilized garrison state.

Nevertheless, if there is an authoritarian regime in the American future, Ronald Reagan is tailored to the image of the friendly fascist.[7] The man would foreclose a widow's mortgage to stimulate her work incentives and eliminate a Social Security pensioner's minimum benefits to restore his self-respect and alleviate his guilt at collecting unearned subsidy. Friendly fascists are amiable individuals, predisposed to tidiness and efficiency. They do not seek to curtail anyone's liberty, they do favor better exchanges of information among law enforcement authorities and, perhaps, national identification cards. If America is to preserve freedom against Soviet threats, disloyal or merely misguided Americans must be searched out and neutralized. The right to strike is in most circumstances a cherished worker option but not when it is illegally taken up by air traffic controllers and, perhaps somewhat later, workers producing vital defense matériel. No one is brazen enough to deny that a free press is a bastion of democracy. Should it also be licensed to print classified government documents?

Should the United States slide into fascism, it will be sanctioned, to adapt Huey Long's cynical aphorism, in the name of anticommunism and as the surest means of preserving free markets and the Bill of Rights. Freedom and security sometimes actually are and more frequently are asserted to be, in conflict. A public sufficiently frightened by violent criminals and internal subversives next door and the Soviets and international terrorists abroad might readily endorse measures to alleviate their apprehensions.

As a sequel to the economic experiment in progress, the national security state requires the support of the business community. Fortunately, the interests and political attitudes of its members frequently diverge and clash. At least since the 1920s,[8]

---

[7]My City University colleague Bertram Gross coined this memorable term.

[8]As Calvin Coolidge's secretary of commerce, Herbert Hoover promoted the mild planning entailed by promulgation of national product specifications and standards. As president, he sponsored the Reconstruction Finance Corporation mostly to bail out nearly bankrupt banks, railroads, and public utilities. Any capital allocation device, however primitive, is a planning tool capable of extension from the nearly defunct to the more wholesome sectors of the economy.

a segment of business opinion has preferred planning to the untidy operations of disorganized markets. Roosevelt's National Recovery Administration (NRA) featured industrial self-government. For a time, the large corporations which dominated administration of the NRA pricing standards favored this de facto partnership between government and industry.

Indeed as far back as World War I, the business community has sanctioned emergency planning and sent corporate leaders to Washington to administer rationing, priorities, and controls over wage and prices. Emergency is a word that justifies government actions otherwise opposed as contrary to free market principles. It was none other than David Stockman who urged Ronald Reagan to declare a state of economic emergency as his initial presidential act. *Business Week*'s appeal for the reindustrialization of America[9] emanated from the throats of sophisticated friends of the corporate sector alarmed enough by the inadequate performance of the American economy to advocate, as a remedy, considerable amendment of the usual processes by which wages and prices are set. The centerpiece of *Business Week*'s incomes policy was a social compact between business and labor. Its terms included wage restraint and explicit neglect of environmental and minority priorities. Unless rapid economic growth resumed, the editors argued, few resources would be available to alleviate poverty and promote environmental causes in any event.

Business Week did its best to escape the stigma of explicit national planning. It asked the federal government simply to bless détente between management and unions and, for the rest, lighten regulatory burdens upon business. Nonetheless, the magazine's editors implicitly accepted organizational realities denied by genuine supply-siders and monetarists, for no social compact is imaginable in classically competitive markets. In them, sellers are so numerous and the market so fragmented

[9]See the magazine's special issue of June 30, 1980.

that no agreement could be enforced even if it could first be negotiated. In free-market utopias neither large corporations nor national unions exist to exert power over key prices and wage bargains. Prices emerge from the interplay of supply and demand, not from the decisions made by industry price leaders like General Motors and IBM. Wage rates reflect the relationship at any moment between the number of jobs available and the number of people seeking employment.

Any appeal for pricing or wage restraint implicitly accepts the existence and importance of market power. The corollary of power is choice. For corporations, the alternatives may be higher prices and smaller sales or lower prices and larger sales. For unions, bargaining strategy in hard times frequently imposes trade-offs between jobs and income. Whatever their public obeisance to free markets, corporate planners have come to terms with market power.

Rather tentatively, corporate planners have begun to hint that after supply-side economics disappoints its sponsors, a new policy might well take its cue from the manner in which New York City was rescued from bankruptcy in the mid-1970s. In effect, the bankers and corporate leaders took the city into receivership from the politicians and planned its recovery. The planners created two new institutions of control, the Financial Control Board, and the Municipal Assistance Corporation. The first body must sanction the city's budget and its biennial contracts with municipal trade unions. The second sells its own securities, guaranteed by liens on city revenue, as a substitute for direct borrowing by the city. From their beginnings, both of these quasi-governmental inventions have been mixed groups of elected officials and business representatives. No union officials, consumer advocates, or other disturbing elements are eligible.

Felix Rohatyn, the Lazard Frères investment banker credited with playing a key role in the creation and administration of these planning agencies, summarized their tactics in the following words:

New York City was kept out of bankruptcy by a wage freeze, a 20 percent reduction in manpower, shifts in pension costs, a tuition charge at the City University, transit fare increases, and savage cost control, coupled with a variety of state tax cuts, and inflation-driven revenue increases; but it was the lower-income families that got hurt.[10]

Like intelligent European partisans of planning in the corporate interest, Rohatyn worries about social justice as the necessary insurance of social stability. When the natives mutiny, business as usual cannot be conducted. The Reagan experiment, Rohatyn gravely warns, will be "either the last or the next-to-last change in direction we can stand in this century; we may hope that success will make it the last."

His respects paid to a new administration, Rohatyn sketches a design for a "last chance" policy in the event of Reagan failure. It is a planner's blueprint. The United States, despite 1981's oil glut, remains vulnerable to interruptions of OPEC supplies. For that vulnerability, "decontrol" in the administration fashion is no answer. It is neither an "energy policy" nor an indication of awareness of the need for "vastly more drastic measures to provide self-sufficiency," among them planned development of alternatives to fossil fuels and intensified conservation efforts.

For Rohatyn, monetarism is a calamity. He echoes European apprehensions that "important sectors of the economy cannot stand another twelve months of interest rates at or near the present levels." They endanger Western European hopes of recovery and imperil, in the United States, "major industrial firms, some airlines, the entire savings industry, and other financial institutions." Undeviating monetarism threatens "major bankruptcies" capable of setting off a chain of liquidations.

Internationally, economic disorder is even more extreme.

---

[10]From testimony to the House Ways and Means Committee, March 5, 1981, reprinted in the *New York Review of Books,* April 16, 1981, pp. 14, 16.

The strength of the American dollar in alliance with the spread of high interest rates to other countries has caused recession and severe balance-of-payments deficits in Western Europe. As usual, the finances of the Third World are a mess. Its $70 billion balance-of-payments deficit must be "financed by a Western banking system overextended already." Rohatyn worries about loss of control: "A trillion dollars in the Eurodollar market are floating outside of any control, while talk of recycling petrodollars becomes more and more a fairy tale." Our banks have become "hostage" to the swelling debts of developing countries. It is essential that "any U.S. economic program must speak to the international monetary situation." Again laissez faire is no solution.

Within the United States, government ought to respond intelligently to urban and regional difficulties. Without such intervention, the problems of the older cities "will only get worse with unforeseeable but, quite probably, most unpleasant consequences," for "no democracy is workable half rich, half poor." Reagan policies are dead wrong. The budget cuts hit northern states hardest. The "tax cuts will encourage industry to move" and "oil price decontrol and defense increases clearly benefit the Sun Belt."

Nor does Rohatyn expect supposedly free markets to cure inflation which has become intractable precisely because "wages and prices . . . have not responded to economic market forces." Inflation has become "deeply embedded" in part because "pensions and contracts are driven upward by Cost of Living Allotments." These are malfunctions "largely unaffected by the administration program."

As usual, Rohatyn's chosen treatment requires more, not less, government intervention in private markets, to start with "a temporary freeze of wages and prices to deal with inflationary behavior that does not respond to other measures." Incomes policy is the litmus test that separates free marketeers from closet and overt planners. And for a true supply-sider, markets already are either free or shortly will be liberated by deregulation. The supply-sider never ceases to celebrate such markets. In them, prices and wages measure the impulses of autonomous actors, free men and women who fulfill their aspirations in the activities they pursue, the prices they charge, and the wages they accept. Any incomes policy sponsored by government limits individual freedom, distorts the market, and diminishes economic efficiency.

From incomes policy, the downward slope is steep toward public guidance of the investment process. Rohatyn favors "an updated version of the Reconstruction Finance Corporation to deal with companies and industries in difficulties as well as related regional and urban problems." In any economy, investment is the dynamic element, the key to growth, productivity gains, and improvement in living standards. From a free market standpoint inevitably, unfettered markets for capital ought to determine the scale and direction of investment and the price of borrowed funds. To money markets, savers bring such sums as they decide not to spend. In such markets investors borrow the amounts they think they can profitably devote to structures and capital equipment. Interest rates, like other prices, translate into productive action the free choices of independent men and women.

To advocate allocation of investment funds to troubled enterprises, industries, and governmental units is to deny the efficacy of market forces. Those who accept that efficacy know that capital flows as it should in the direction of highest potential profit. For less attractive industries and the regions which harbor them, the news is bad. Investors have weighed their economic prospects against alternatives elsewhere and voted their dollars to ventures in Texas, Taiwan, Hong Kong, Singapore, and other dynamic centers of growth. To reject this verdict, as Rohatyn does, is either to deny that capital markets invariably are competitive and efficient or set above efficiency the political objectives of equity and stability.

Within the business community, the planners are concentrated in the declining Northeast. Whether, in the turbulent internal politics of the business community in the wake of supply-side and monetarist collapse, they will stand a chance against the hard-line national security state advocates powerful in the Sun Belt and the Reagan Administration, is a matter of conjecture.

On many grounds corporate planning is preferable to the national security model. As they define their own interests, the corporate planners concern themselves with poverty, urban blight, and regional decline. They willingly temper the rigors of market capitalism with the protections of the welfare state. Their anxiety about social stability in the United States and elsewhere in the world frequently implies policies to diminish unemployment and improve the situation of struggling minorities. The quest for stability implies also less bellicose attitudes toward the Soviets.

If it comes to pass in the United States, corporate planning, for all its comparative merits, will not resolve the dilemmas of income distribution associated with slow growth. The claims for profit of the corporate sector are likely to exceed the resources that are available without reductions in wages, Social Security benefits, and other protections against the hardships of life. Unless the pace of economic growth considerably accelerates, corporate planners cannot hope to guarantee the social stability necessary to the peaceful pursuit of profit.

Political transitions rarely are tidy events. As supply-side nostrums leave their patient sicker than ever, the sequel is likely to depend on the depth of ideological conviction that inspires the president and his helpers. There is no reason to doubt David Stockman's fervent confidence in the power of incentives, nor, at the Treasury, Undersecretary Beryl Sprinkel's certainty that monetarism is the only answer to economic disorder.

Elsewhere in the administration the ideological temperature is lower. On Wall Street, Treasury Secretary Donald Regan was noted as the highly successful head man at Merrill Lynch. His conversion to the supply side appeared to coincide with his appointment by Mr. Reagan. The White House triumvirate—

Meese, Baker, and Deaver—have strong opinions about the Russians. As far as the economy is concerned, their instincts are those of self-made millionaires. Like other accumulators of wealth, they dislike taxes and regulation. It is doubtful whether these normal entrepreneurial reactions are linked to the doctrinal devotion of the Stockmans, Kemps, and Gilders.

The president himself has been known to temper ideology with political expediency. Free market principles did not dissuade Mr. Reagan from continuation of tobacco subsidies in deference to Senator Helms. Nor did his desire to prune the budget and get government out of investment markets prevent him from including money for the Clinch River breeder reactor in salute to Senator Howard Baker.

IV

If, in the next few years, we avoid the menace of right-wing authoritarianism, the terms of political discussion are likely to derive from the nature of necessary public intervention. Corporate-dominated planning will naturally establish priorities for high returns to investors, favorable tax treatment of large incomes, limited wage improvements, and continuation of present patterns of income and wealth distribution.

Thus far in the United States the voice of a less inequalitarian, decentralized, socialist alternative is weak. In France, the socialist government of François Mitterand appears to be conducting an experiment in such a spirit. Mitterand is vigorously shaking up a society far more traditionally in the grip of its bureaucracy than the United States.

Mitterand is playing a song unexpectedly popular in his own country and almost never heard in the United States. The lyrics are a libretto for a socialist opera: heavier taxes on the rich, nationalization of selected banks and corporations, higher minimum wages, public jobs for the unemployed, new legal rights for unions, enlistment of labor as an important partner of government, and decentralization of government. As a much smaller and weaker economy than the United States, France is vulnerable to conscientious sabotage from its own capitalists and their American allies. If Mitterand fails, it is much more likely to be the consequence of such sabotage than of the defects in his approach.

The immediate political prospects for an American democratic Left are visibly poor. Yet it is hard to believe that the failure of the Reagan approach will not shake up our stagnant politics. On the optimistic view, that continued economic adversity will evoke a revival of radicalism on the democratic Left, I shall conclude my depressing journey through Reagan country with a brief comment on the lessons to be learned from the short life of Great Society liberalism.

In 1980, the Democratic party deserved to lose, which of course is not to say that the Republicans merited their triumph. In his four frustrating years as president, Jimmy Carter failed to redeem party pledges to federalize welfare, create a comprehensive health system, and restore high levels of employment. When growth screeched to a halt, the Great Society became a luxury too expensive for the wallets of hard-pressed Americans of moderate income. Blue-collar workers in particular were outraged at the notion, by no means completely justified, that their tax dollars were going in large numbers to poor people not much better off than they themselves and much less inclined to scramble for jobs.

Their reaction identifies a major weakness of the Great Society, its focus upon low-income groups. As I observed earlier, it is an old adage in the social welfare community that programs for poor people are poor programs. They tend to be underfunded, overadministered, and resented by the public as overindulgent to the lazy and work-shy. On the evidence, they are tolerated for as long as general prosperity improves the incomes of most of the public and an occasional tax reduction allays anger at welfare waste.

The most successful social programs are universal. Social

Security pensions and Medicare are available to almost every American who has lived long enough to be eligible. They are also enormously popular. Public housing in England has been far more successful than in the United States in good measure because "council housing" is available without a means test. Medicaid exemplifies the problem. In a most important way, Medicaid has been an enormous success story. It has increased medical services for the working poor as well as the welfare population. Families who rarely benefitted from the attention of physicians now had them available at no cost. However, families with only slightly higher incomes than the eligibility cutoff point were compelled to rely upon incomplete Blue Cross protection and pay a substantial portion of their own medical bills.

It was a situation bound to change. Either, as the administration has sought to do, Medicaid is reduced in coverage or it is transformed into universal health coverage. Democratic failure between 1976 and 1980 to move in this direction revealed a second limitation of Great Society liberalism. Medicaid was enormously expensive. Each year hospital costs and physicians' fees rose far faster than general inflation rates. Good liberals flinched at the estimates of enlarging this fiscal monstrosity.

Liberals were timid. The inference they should have drawn from the Medicaid experience was simple but politically challenging. If public money is paid to an entrepreneurial health sector, that sector will increase its services but it will do so at an inordinate cost. Health providers did well on Medicaid money. The health sector must be restructured and the entrepreneurial model junked before universal health care can be financed. Salaried physicians, community-based Health Maintenance Organizations, and a single set of publicly supported hospitals, are possible elements of comprehensive health care.

Effective liberalism in the sense of pursuit of the traditional agenda of full employment, broader social protections, and fairer treatment of vulnerable groups, will in American terms seem radical, for it will require incomes policy, industrial re-structuring, and direction of investment, all dodged by liberals when the going was good.

I do not despair. American politics are volatile and unpredictable. Few expected Franklin Roosevelt to preside over the most creative political period in American history. Not many thought that Lyndon Johnson would do more for civil rights than Abraham Lincoln. Moreover, I share just a little of the economist's faith in the importance of self-interest. Supply-side economics and monetarism promote the fortunes of small numbers of Americans. As that conclusion spreads, men and women who voted hopefully for Ronald Reagan will seek a better representative of their interests and a platform quite different from this administration's.

To that platform I now turn.

8

revival
on the left

Carter's peanuts were more
nourishing than Reagan's jellybeans.

Legend on a placard displayed
by a marching machinist,
SOLIDARITY DAY IN WASHINGTON,
September 19, 1981

On a cool, cloudy day in September 1981, at least 260,000 men
and women assembled on the Washington Mall to protest the
policies of the Reagan Administration. There were environ-
mentalists, solar energy enthusiasts, male and female partisans
of the Equal Rights Amendment, Gray Panthers, and, on the
sidelines, occasional hawkers of instant revolution. But blue-
collar workers dominated the scene. Some had driven a day and
a night from Michigan and Wisconsin. A Maine delegation had
endured nineteen hours in buses from Bangor to Washington.
Others had taken their cars from Seattle to Vancouver to catch
Canadian flights as a mark of support for American air traffic
controllers. In the crowd were 30,000 sheet-metal workers,
carpenters, electricians, and other building trades craftsmen,

many of whom had voted for Ronald Reagan a brief ten months earlier.

Ignoring their outburst of *lèse majesté,* Ronald Reagan spent the weekend at Camp David. But the following Thursday, addressing the nation on all major television channels, he supplied an implicit commentary. Intent upon protecting both the Pentagon and, for the time being, Social Security pensioners, he offered the dreary prospect of a second round of budget cuts, targeted according to the precedent of the first expenditure slashes on profligate welfare families, food stamp gourmets, and other unneedy Americans.[1] Here was the Reagan we have come to know, if not necessarily admire. However, the Great Communicator was curiously defensive in tone. He could not have expected low-income Americans to applaud the worsening of their condition, but the mutual alliance in disaffection between them and Wall Street must have been as unwelcome as it was unanticipated. No wonder the president was constrained to remind his constituents that they must be patient and wait for the tax cuts to work their magical spell.

In all probability, Solidarity Day signaled a gathering mobilization against the concerted assault on trade unions, consumers, women, children, the working poor, and the elderly. When the 260,000 assembled in midafternoon near the Capitol, they listened to a message of resistance from Coretta Scott King and NAACP head Benjamin Hooks, representing the civil rights community, and Lane Kirkland, an improbable convert to mass action, speaking for organized labor. None of the demonstrators could have expected his presence to influence the White House. Among the politicians, their immediate targets were dispirited congressional Democrats. As usual, however, the most important impact of such a mass gathering was

---

[1]Hinting darkly at bureaucratic sabotage, the Department of Agriculture withdrew, for some modification, their school lunch guidelines which defined pickle relish and catsup as vegetables, jam as fruit, and cake as bread. The retreat was a mildly encouraging sign that ridicule penetrates the thickest of political skins.

upon the participants, many of whom realized with a shiver of pleasant astonishment that they had company in their detestation of Reagan policies.

The AFL-CIO embraces a diminishing minority of the labor force. It is perhaps less than coincidental that it has been hawkish in foreign affairs and unimaginative in organizational strategy. Nevertheless, the AFL-CIO has consistently been our most important institutional advocate of full employment, comprehensive health care, civil rights, decent standards of social services, and the rest of the liberal Democratic agenda. In the United States, a serious resurgence of progressive forces must be based on massive recruiting from organized labor.[2]

Inevitably, the message from the podium on Solidarity Day stressed resistance to the administration's advocacy of the remaining features of the New Right agenda—environmental devastation, dismantling of safeguards to worker health and safety, retreat from sexual and racial equality, and destruction of the New Deal and Great Society. Opposition to evil by itself is inadequate. Badly needed is a coherent program, one that is responsive to the interests and needs of the majority of Americans who will gradually realize that they can expect little benefit from policies blatantly contrived to make the rich richer and almost everybody else worse off.

This has not been a cheerful book. I have not ignored, on the contrary I may have overemphasized, the grim plausibility of a garrison state or a venture in corporate planning as the next episode in conservative retention of power. Yet, one should no more indulge in despair than wallow in utopian fantasies. American politics is notoriously volatile. As the disarray of the economy becomes a cause for distress among increasing numbers of Americans and appreciation of the inequities and ineffi-

---

[2]Labor is no more monolithic in ideology than corporate America. For some time, ferment within the ranks of the machinists, autoworkers, and state and local employees has reflected the search for new ideas and policies on the part of leaders like William Winpisinger, Douglas Fraser, and Jerry Wurf.

ciencies of administration tactics spreads, there is hope that an outcome different from those suggested in the previous chapter is still a political possibility.

AN AGENDA FOR THE LEFT

The time is ripe for revival on the Left, that spectrum extending from mainstream Democrats to democratic socialists. Lacking thus far has been a credible agenda, objectives and programs consistent with a politics at another state of advance in the Great Society. Here is one partisan's attempt to sketch an approach to renewed progress.

The Reagan triumph in 1980 owed less to the contents of the Republican platform than to the failure of the Carter presidency, a point worth recalling when assessing the scope of support for this administration and its policies. That failure was in part the consequence of bad luck—the Iranian hostage crisis, the second oil price shock in 1979, and the continued erosion of the American share of world trade. Carter was unfortunate in an additional and politically fatal respect. As I have elsewhere in this volume explained, New Deal and Great Society liberalism, honorable though their record has been in many ways, was certainly by 1976 a force that had depleted its intellectual capital. More than Carter's inept handling of a Democratic Congress is to blame for the failure to advance toward broader health coverage, federalization of welfare, and full employment. Liberals in Congress came to realize that, within the context of substantially undisturbed market capitalism, full employment, equitable welfare reform, and universal medical benefits were just too expensive to be contemplated in an era of sluggish economic growth and endemic inflation.

Liberal revival will accordingly be founded on initiatives radical in appearance for Americans, if not for Europeans. The place to begin is with recognition of the dominant position of the large corporation as employer, guarantor of community and regional prosperity, shaper of national investment policy, and manipulator of public opinion and electoral processes.

Credible pursuit of full employment, reconstruction of urban communities, stable prices, and increased equity in the distribution of income and wealth requires effective political control of corporate policy and, in particular, regulation of investment. Just as corporate planners like Felix Rohatyn contemplate the use of a redesigned Reconstruction Finance Corporation to shore up faltering banks and corporations in the distressed Northeast and industrial Midwest,[3] planners on the democratic left could direct capital toward defense contractors who agree to convert their facilities to the making of buses and subway cars, developers who are willing to construct housing for low and moderate income families, medical entrepreneurs whose Health Maintenance Organizations serve inner city and distressed rural constituencies, and local groups who engage in energy production from renewable sources.[4]

Investment is the key element in economic growth. Who controls investment dominates the economy and defines the limits of political action. But it is less important whether a progressive national administration nationalizes some major banks in the French fashion than that it control the terms, amounts, and direction of the flow of credit to borrowers. Public control of investment need not, and ought not, involve the rigidities of excessive centralization. Nothing either in principle or administrative practice will prevent a National Investment Authority, should one be created, from delegating funds and responsibility for their allocation to regional subsidiaries who

[3] There is an unbenign side to Rohatyn's version of planning. Before his RFC grants credit to an enterprise, its workers would be required to make substantial sacrifices in wages, benefits, and work rule protections, on the model, explicitly favored by Rohatyn, of the events in New York City after the 1975 flirtation with municipal bankruptcy.
[4] The machinists' union, imaginatively guided by William ("Wimpy") Winpisinger, had designed concrete specifications for conversion of defense plants to civilian production. Wimpy, a self-described "seat-of-the-pants socialist," is a member of the Democratic Socialist Organizing Committee. Nevertheless, his members overwhelmingly re-elected him for a new term of office in 1981. Possibly the rank and file are less conservative than conventional stereotypes insist they are.

will be encouraged to foster community-based cooperatives, church-sponsored housing, and union-managed enterprises.

Even now, of course, investment is financed in the public sector from tax revenue and in the private sector by voluntary savings. Most of the latter is furnished by the small minority whose incomes exceed $50,000. A dangerously high fraction of private saving is wasted in speculation, tax shelters, mergers, and corporate takeovers. The American economy in the last decade has not been afflicted by a capital shortage. Its growth has been sabotaged by misdirection of available funds.

The diagnosis implies the nature of the remedy. It comes in two parts. As fractions of total investment, the share of the private sector should diminish while that of the public sector increases. The funds for public investment should be extracted from much heavier taxes upon the income and property of affluent Americans. Such revision of the tax code is clearly equitable, and it is also efficient. The funds diverted from speculative and socially useless private investment will be the sources of renewal in housing, public transportation, and health care— three important areas in which private enterprise has conspicuously failed to meet the needs of many, indeed most, Americans.

Control of inflation is as vital to a progressive program as direction of investment. Inflation typically afflicts wage earners, the working poor, those who depend on private pensions, and the welfare population far more gravely than more prosperous individuals and families. As intelligent conservatives have begun to realize, recession as an inflation cure is more painful than the condition it is designed to alleviate. As unemployment soars, profits decline and markets shrink. The rewards of diminished inflation are excruciatingly slow to manifest themselves.

Thus, after two and a half years of determined efforts to restrain the growth of money and credit and complementary actions to curtail public expenditure, Margaret Thatcher's Great Britain (in the autumn of 1981) endured 12.4 percent unemployment, an echo of the 1930s, and an inflation rate of 11.5 percent—almost identical to the figure that greeted British Conservatives when they took office—spreading business bankruptcies, disordered securities markets, and a weakening currency. To the surprise of no one, public opinion polls reported that if Mrs. Thatcher had been imprudent enough to call a general election, her party would be swept out of office.[5]

I have reiterated the lessons of recent experience. Monetarist remedies do not work. No more satisfactory are supply-side fixes shakily predicated upon elusive investment booms and resulting tidal waves of cheap goods and services. Both nostrums rely heavily on the operation of free markets guided by invisible hands inoperative within the lifetime of the oldest inhabitant. Monetarists wistfully assume that recession will exert effective downward pressure upon wages and prices. Supply-siders just know in their hearts that increased saving will translate into productive investment. Their faith is touching, but their works are inadequate.

In the United States there are some genuinely competitive markets. For the most part, they are located in retailing and in a handful of shrinking, older industries such as clothing, textiles, and commercial printing. Most sectors of the economy register the force of concentrated market power—Pentagon defense contractor communities of interest, price leadership by General Motors in the auto industry, control of interest rates by interplay between the Federal Reserve and its constituency of major money market banks, alliances between corporate farmers and the Department of Agriculture, tidy arrangements between public utilities and the public service commissions that "regulate" them, and so on. In the words, not of John Kenneth Galbraith, but of our friend Felix Rohatyn, "the price of our energy is not freely set, nor is the price of our food, or the price at which we borrow money. Free markets are clearly desirable but we do not in fact live in a free-market economy and never

---

[5]See the *New York Times*, September 26, 1981, p. 32.

will."[6] Because important markets are dominated by one or two major operators, the prices charged are enormously resistant to recession. As auto and steel producers have repeatedly demonstrated, they can choose between low volume-high price and high volume-low price strategies when demand falters. Almost invariably, they opt for higher prices and smaller sales.

To anyone whose mind has not been clouded by graduate economic training, it is obvious that this is not what Adam Smith or Milton Friedman had in mind as a model of competitive behavior. In the ideal markets of theoretical legend, merchants and manufacturers, confronted by fleeing customers, reduce prices to whatever fraction of their original figure might be needed to lure buyers back into stores and showrooms.

Prices are the sources of wages, rent, executive salaries, and dividends. In effect, the private sector frequently, either overtly or through clandestine cooperation with government, operates an incomes policy. It imposes much of its costs upon laid-off workers. It is biased toward inflation and against efficiency. And it is irresponsible: it eludes control by elected officials and, most of the time, escapes serious examination by the media.

In short, the electorate and its representatives cannot choose between free markets and institutional guidance of prices and incomes, as supply-siders and monetarists misleadingly assert. The realistic alternatives are political definition of permissible private sector conduct or acceptance of the existing pattern of corporate domination. To couch the choice in slightly different terms, Americans can allow prices and incomes to be determined by private political actors or they can substitute, for anonymous company presidents, elected officials responsive to their constituents and replaceable by them at regularly scheduled elections.

---

[6]Quoted in *Working Papers*, September/October, 1981, p. 45.

In a democratically planned polity, there is a permanent need for legislatively defined price and incomes standards, simply because powerful private interests will otherwise sabotage the best-laid of progressive plans. The emphasis of an equitable incomes policy should be upon prices instead of wages. That strategic choice is more important than the control device chosen, whether the promulgation of specific standards for allowable price increases or an experiment with a variety of tax benefits for good price behavior or tax penalties for the opposite.

Unions have customarily resisted controls out of a justifiable apprehension that wage restraints would turn out to be far more effective than parallel checks upon prices and nonwage incomes. For one thing, employers joyfully cooperate with the controllers to restrain wage improvement. But, if the key components of the cost of living—food staples, clothing, home heating fuel, public transportation, major appliances, autos, and credit charges—were controlled, pressure for inflationary wage bargains would appreciably diminish. Cost-of-living escalators written into union contracts would cease to propel inflation. At contract renewal time, union negotiators could bargain for benefits consistent with potential productivity gains, leaving aside demands for protection against anticipated inflation or compensation for the erosion of previously negotiated improvements eroded by inflation. Moreover, price restraints in semimonopolistic portions of the private economy serve the equitable purpose of diminishing extortionate profits and executive emoluments.

There is a last point. Critics of controls invariably cite an asserted need for an enormous bureaucracy. So long, to the contrary, as controls apply exclusively to large financial and industrial units that now set prices privately, no large bureaucracy is required. Regulators proliferate only when controls are unnecessarily extended to retailing. Retailers do compete. It is their suppliers of credit and merchandise who frequently do not.

FULL EMPLOYMENT

A major objective of progressive policies is a job for every man, woman, and teen-ager who credibly seeks work. Unemployment is as universally deplored as it is privately welcomed by conservative politicians and corporate employers. The brutal fact is that unemployment at "moderate" 7 or 8 percent rates (the recent American performance) confers many benefits upon the prosperous and truly affluent. If everyone were employed, extraordinarily high wages would have to be paid to toilers in restaurant kitchens, laundries, filling stations, and other unpleasant work environments. Whenever decent employment at living wages is available, it is exceedingly difficult to coax young men and women into our volunteer armed services. (Yet, without volunteers, how can the children of the middle and upper classes be spared the rigors of the draft?)

Unemployment calms unions and moderates wage demands. Threats to shut down or shift mills and assembly plants coerce workers into acceptance of wage freezes or actual wage cuts and unfavorable revisions of work rules. When men and women fear for their jobs, they work harder and gripe less. In more dignified language, absenteeism declines and productivity accelerates. Better still, from the managerial perspective, factory and office employees, alert to potential layoffs and shutdowns, are much less likely than in better times to nag union leaders and employers to make their jobs more interesting and less menacing to health and individual safety. It is more than a coincidence that in Sweden, where job enrichment and plant democracy have proceeded furthest, unemployment for several decades has been held by public policy at close to zero. American employers protect themselves from dangerous extensions of Swedish experiments to their own operations by keeping the industrial reserve army at full strength. Unions, their members, and employers all know that it is jobs that count and that their scarcity keeps wages down and other items on the bargaining agenda impossible of realization.

Nor is this yet the whole of the matter. The hunger of communities and regions for jobs and tax revenue has encouraged major private employers to extort an endless assortment of valuable concessions from local and state governments, either as blackmail to retain existing installations or bribes to attract new ones. Few major corporations pay their fair share of property taxes, and even before the advent of Ronald Reagan, propaganda financed by oil, steel, chemical, auto, paper, and other malefactors noticeably slowed the pace of environmental regulation.

By contrast, full employment on a sustained and assured basis—market capitalism American style can tolerate a spell of full employment in wartime emergencies so long as all parties understand that it is temporary—can't help but embarrass movers and shakers in our traditional plutocracy. For full employment is the most efficient agent of equitable income redistribution politically conceivable within the parameters of market capitalism. Full employment sucks into the labor force individuals who now strive desperately to survive on welfare, food stamps, Social Security, and unemployment compensation. Full employment improves wages for low-paid workers whose financial situation is only slightly less precarious than that of the unemployed. It is a particular boon to blacks, Hispanics, teenagers,[7] and women, last hired in good times and first fired in recessions. A protracted period of full employment would substantially narrow the existing indefensibly wide differentials between the earnings of these groups and those of white males. In times of layoffs, contraction, or the stagflation of the last

[7]In August 1981, for the first time since the statistics began to be collected, black teen-age unemployment exceeded 50 percent (almost surely an undercount). The word from the Reagan White House was advice to wait patiently for the president's program to get the economy moving again.

decade, affirmative action (even without the tender attentions of this administration's Department of Justice) becomes a mockery.

Without full employment, the odds are against restructuring the economy away from emphasis upon weapons procurement and massive, wasteful highway construction like New York's Westway, and toward mass transit, public housing, community health facilities, and repair in the older cities of crumbling bridges, sewers, parks, subways, and local roads.

Because full employment entails radical consequences, it has been approximated only during the Korean and Vietnam wars, the only time in the third of a century since the Employment Act of 1946 stated as a national objective the achievement and maintenance of a high level of employment. As earlier recorded, the Humphrey-Hawkins Balanced Growth and Full Employment Act of 1978 fell into the national memory hole at the moment it became law.

Inflation has been the usual pretext, and as such endorsed by most appropriately credentialed economists, for consistent evasion of the legislative mandate to place full employment high on the list of domestic priorities. Inflation impelled Jimmy Carter, in the spring of 1980, to cooperate with the Federal Reserve to shove the nation into one of the sharpest, though briefest, recessions in business cycle history. Inflation constitutes the Reagan Administration's justification for accepting indefinite continuation of national unemployment at heights which, a generation ago, spelled political crisis. Eisenhower presided over three recessions during his eight years of office, but in the worst month of the most serious of the trio, unemployment was measured at 7.6 percent, a number now calmly interpreted as normal and, on occasion, in the musings of conservative economists, identical with a definition of full employment consonant with conservative preferences for frightened employees and weak unions.

I cannot overemphasize the necessity of equitable inflation control. Unless well-designed incomes policies restore price stability, full employment will remain elusive. In its absence, sensible redirection of the economy toward humane goals will continue to be a fantasy.

THE REST OF THE WORLD

This has been a polemic about the impact of Ronald Reagan and his helpers upon the United States. However, administration policies have also gravely damaged advanced economies and the developing world. The high interest rates that have distorted our own economic activity have spread to Western Europe and Canada and in so doing have impeded West German recovery and damaged prospects for the Mitterand regime's ambitious plans for France. They have encouraged Mrs. Thatcher to persevere in her calamitous mismanagement of the British economy.

Washington's maneuvers have been far more menacing to those portions of the Third World that have no oil of their own. When domestic programs are savagely mutilated, Congress inevitably slashes still more destructively at foreign aid. Worse still, the administration guides such funds as Congress authorizes away from even mildly left-wing regimes and toward hardline, authoritarian, anticommunist governments.

The administration has exacerbated the debasement of American aid policy by pressure upon international lending agencies to tighten loan terms and show favor for free-market regimes. In tandem, these destructive alterations of past practice court breakdown of the precarious structure of international payments and may contribute to worldwide financial crisis. Since OPEC's 1973 revision of the globe's pecking order, the international economy has been as delicately poised on the brink of breakdown as it was just before the Great Crash of 1929. The economic historian Charles P. Kindleberger summarized the earlier situation as one in which "Germany owes reparations to Britain and France and commercial debts to the United States; Britain owes to the United States about what it receives from Germany, and is owed war debts from France; France is to receive the lion's share of reparations, well in excess of its war debts to Britain and the United States."[8]

During the booming 1920s, no American leader admitted that Allied war debts payable to the United States were linked in fact, though not in law, to the continued flow of German reparations to France and England. Nor did politicians and bankers concede that the only way Germans could pay up was with funds borrowed from American bankers and investors. As soon as the Americans tired of pumping capital into Germany, the Germans were certain to default on their reparations obligations, followed quickly by the British and French on their debts to the United States. When these possibilities materialized, mutual reprisals and recriminations promptly poisoned the atmosphere and sabotaged efforts here and in Europe to promote recovery. Most momentous of all, Hitler's path to power was eased and World War II rendered inevitable.

In the 1980s, it is fortunate that neither war debts nor reparations complicate international relations. However, as a substitute, the continuing strains inflicted by OPEC on oil importers ought to remind those equipped with historical memory of the last occasion on which the world economy parted at the seams. The so-called recycling problem involves vast flows of funds from oil importers to oil exporters and from the latter to deposits or investments in advanced communities or the oil-poor countries of the developing world. The World Bank estimated the 1979 deficit of developing nations without oil at $42 billion. That sum has risen steadily in spite of temporary moderation of petroleum prices in 1981. Until now all parties have financed oil imports without actual calamity mainly because OPEC has recycled many billions of dollars of oil revenue as deposits in Chase, Citibank and other money market institutions here and

---

[8]See Charles P. Kindleberger, *The World in Depression: 1929–1939,* University of California Press (1973), p. 27.

in Western Europe. In turn, they have extended large loans to poor nations.

These commercial credits indispensably complement inadequate lending by international organizations, primarily the World Bank and the International Monetary Fund, which in recent years have filled at most a fifth of the deficits in the accounts of impoverished, oil-importing nations in Africa, Latin America, and elsewhere. During the 1920s, World War I's victors excluded from their domestic market German exports that might have paid for reparations without loans from America. In our own day, rich countries seem equally reluctant to allow Third World merchandise to threaten jobs and profits, yet another malignant consequence of tolerating persistent unemployment. Under the circumstances, larger and larger new loans are as essential to the Third World as they were to Germany in the 1920s.

Dangerous possibilities abound. American and European banks may decide to swallow large losses and pull out of the poorer and less stable countries of the Third World. Large debtors may default. For either political or financial reasons, the dominant Arab participants in OPEC may withdraw deposits from Western banks. One or more of the latter might close its doors and trigger a series of related bankruptcies. Any one of these events would produce grave repercussions that would severely test the adaptive capacities of central banks, governments, and international agencies.

Most of the calamities of conjecture never occur. Such consolation as this platitude conveys must be tempered by an awareness of the feebleness of cooperative attempts to resolve foreseeable problems and the ideological intransigence of American policymakers. In the remainder of this century, global economic prosperity hinges upon difficult choices. Will developed countries set aside intramural squabbles and collaborate in response to OPEC and the Third World? Will OPEC, filled with vivid memories of grievances against rich countries and equipped with little altruistic feeling for poor neighbors, shape its pricing and investment policies with the wisdom appropriate for an important creditor? It is conceivable that looming economic and political disorder will invite unprecedented international cooperation. It is not an outcome on which to bet one's last ingot.

DEMOCRATIC PLANNING

Although it may seem unnecessary to say this once again, mandatory incomes policy, political direction of investment, redistributive taxation, and full employment policies demand coherent, democratic planning. Such planning raises a series of issues likely to be resolved only by experience. With desperate brevity, I note four.

The first is the relation between central direction and local control, an issue that almost defines the generational difference between the Old and the New Left. The Old Left is fond of coordination from the center and their juniors, heirs of the movements of the 1960s, tend to be strongly committed to communal, cooperative, and union based endeavors. Solutions are likely to be unexpected and inventive. Suffice it here to say that even a centralized investment authority could experiment with the financing of small, decentralized enterprises as well as larger national projects. Small is no more universally beautiful than big is necessarily efficient.

Whether factories and retail establishments are publicly, privately, cooperatively, or union owned, a second significant question concerns the kind and extent of worker control, a road down which Yugoslavia has traveled furthest and one that, by autumn 1981, Polish Solidarity seemed eager to explore.

The fruits of ownership and control are income claims to output. What is the appropriate pattern of distribution in a progressive community? Economists habitually fret over the asserted trade-offs between equity and efficiency. No society has operated for very long on the basis of equality of reward. Yet the issue allows for empirical experiment. I am disposed to echo the sociologist Herbert Gans's response to the query, "How much equality?" with "More." More implies that gaps between rich and poor should be narrowed until it is evident that incentives are too meager to evoke effort and ambition.

There is finally the issue of scale. Is small so preferable on noneconomic grounds that even when the efficiencies favor large units, smaller ones are to be preferred as offering more chances of self-management and greater variety?

Nothing here proposed is novel. In Scandinavia, Austria, Great Britain, France, Germany, Yugoslavia, and Canada, the generally accepted commonplaces of public policy include active labor market policy, universal health coverage, incomes standards, and public intervention into strategic private investment decisions. The American fixation upon private market solutions to public problems is an aberration even in other capitalist societies.

THE PROSPECT BEFORE US

Particularly in the preceding chapter, I have emphasized the authoritarian tendencies in American popular and political culture. Yet there is much that is democratic and egalitarian in American experience and tradition: the assurance of political equality contained in the Bill of Rights, the Fourteenth Amendment, and the civil rights legislation of the 1960s. American political history registers continuing conflict between fundamental law, which asserts that all men and women are equal as citizens, and the tremendous disparities of income and wealth that translate into similar differences in political influence and personal advantage.

It is clear that the Reagan dispensation has tilted the balance still more in the direction of market-generated inequality and diminished the efficacy of legal guarantees of equality which, in the sunshine of the Great Society, were enhanced by legal services' attorneys and sympathetic judicial interpretations.

Americans, like other human beings, crave fair treatment. As the Department of Justice continues to withdraw from civil rights enforcement, as the president continues to appoint anti-union members to the National Labor Relations Board, as the amended tax code even more outrageously indulges corporations and wealthy individuals, as the victims of industrial disease and preventable accidents endure their disabilities on smaller benefits, as fragile protections against illness, unemployment, and old age are one by one dismantled, the sense of individual outrage will seek political expression.

Time is not on President Reagan's side. The damage done by Congress in 1981 will blight many lives in 1982 and afterwards. On Solidarity Day, the democratic left may indeed have begun to mobilize against policies and attitudes deeply offensive to this country's noblest aspirations. Sooner than the pessimists among us have thought possible, progress may resume toward the fuller democracy of libertarian socialism. If such is the shape of events in the near future, those of us who have spent our lives and energies on the democratic left will have reason to thank Ronald Reagan.

index

ABOUT THE AUTHOR

Robert Lekachman is currently Distinguished Professor of Economics at Lehman College in The City University of New York. He received both his A.B. and Ph. D. from Columbia University, and is the author of numerous books including *The Age of Keynes, Inflation,* and most recently *Capitalism for Beginners* (Pantheon).